HOW TO WRITE YOUR BOOK

"the Editor"
Ms. Edi Tor

"the Publisher"
Mr. I. M. Publisher

"the Writer"
Ms. Iwanna B. Writer

From an Idea to YOUR PUBLISHED STORY

as narrated by
The Three Wise Guides

Bobbi Madry & Francine Barish-Stern

 Golden Quill Press

www.goldenquillpress.com

Published By Golden Quill Press
a division of Barish-Stern Ltd.
P O Box 83
Troutville, VA 24175

Copyright © 2018
Bobbi Madry & Francine Barish-Stern

ISBN 0-9676256-4-5

All rights reserved, except for appropriate quotes in reviews or scholarly works. Printed in the United States of America. No part of this publication may be reproduced, stored in a retrieval system or transmitted in any form or by any means, electronic, mechanical, photocopying, recording or other without the written permission of the publisher.,

Interior Design by Kenneth A. Bray, Creations Troutville VA.

Special Offer
A FREE E-GIFT
From Golden Quill Press

The publishers of *How To Write Your Book* and *CODE 47 to BREV Force*

Want to give you a FREE Gift as a Thank You for purchasing
How to Write Your Book,

Read *Code 47 to BREV Force Cracko* e-book for FREE

Reading BREV Force will demonstrate how the advice given throughout *How To Write Your Book, was used* and will help you better implement the tools described for your writing journey

Receive Your FREE E-Gift Today

Email: info@goldenquillpress.com

Send your name, email and proof of purchase for *How To Write Your Book* and your FREE E GIFT, Code 47 to BREV Force- CRACKO in ebook format will be on its way!*
(*please state if you have an e-book format preference)

If you have any questions or comments, please feel free to email us at:
info@goldenquillpress.com

TABLE OF CONTENTS

	Introduction	1 - 5
Writing Map 1	Planning Your Writing Journey	6 - 16
Writing Map 2	Preparing To Write	17 - 23
Writing Map 3	Fleshing Out Your Story	24 - 30
Writing Map 4	Locations, Settings and Time	31 - 39
Writing Map 5	Getting on the Road to Your Plot	40 - 47
Writing Map 6	Constructing Your Story	48 - 60
Writing Map 7	Looking through the Rear View Mirror	61 - 66
Writing Map 8	Mechanic--ism's of Writing	67 - 81
Writing Map 9	Character's Speak Up	82 - 94
Writing Map 10	Your Writing Style	95 - 103
Writing Map 11	Finishing With A Flair	104 - 112
Writing Map 12	Take Your Story To Market	113 - 131
	Glossary	132 - 138
	Final Word From Our Authors	139
	Author Biographies	140

Bio for The Three Wise Guides

Ms. Iwanna B. Writer had always dreamed of being a successful writer. She started as a young child sending stories to contests and one day after years of submissions she finally received a letter saying, "Congratulation Writer- You Have Won 1st Prize in our Nationwide Writing Contest."

When she eventually saw her story published she knew she would never stop writing. Whether it was short stories, journal entries that turned into stories or just ideas pulled from the depths of her imagination, she wrote and wrote and wrote.

By her teen years she had a portfolio of published stories and decided it was time to tackle her first novel. Mrs. Writer found this road much harder to navigate, but after many more years, she did finally have a finished manuscript. She eagerly sent her work out to publishers, and then spent almost as much time sifting through rejections. Finally, after all her persistence, she did a contract and got to hold her published book in her hand.

ADVICE From Ms. Iwanna B. Writer: *Everyone says, 'I want to write a book,' but most people never do. If you have a desire to write, don't let anything stop you. When you finish writing, congratulate yourself on completing that first huge step. But don't stop there, keep going until it gets read!*

Ms. Edi Tor is one of the most respected editors in the industry, but her success didn't just happen overnight. She was a magazine writer for years. One day the home and garden editor took ill and the boss asked her to step in.

She tackled the assignment by first making a list of the best editor's comments she had ever gotten on her article drafts. Next, she devised her own unique system. By the end of the day all the articles for Home and Garden were edited, revised and ready for print. The boss was so impressed, Ms. Tor was promoted to chief editor and the rest is history. Her system of editing is now being taught in college writing courses and journalism schools.

ADVICE From Ms. Edi Tor: *Writing is a step by step process. The work must be well crafted, interesting and capture the reader's attention. But, once written, a story needs professional editing to make it reader worthy!*

Mr. I. M. Publisher took the long way around to in his career. He was a writer of many genres, who evolved into a writer/editor. After several years he realized he enjoyed working on other writer's work more than on his own. He rose up through the ranks and one day the opportunity came to pitch a story he was very excited about. None of his fellow editors or publishers saw what he did and the story remained unpublished, until one day he decided to publish the writer's work himself. He started his own company and today he's known for publishing outside the box.

ADVICE From Mr. I. M. Publisher: *There are so many great stories out there that never see publication of any type. They wind up in bottom drawers, or worse, in the garbage. If a writer took time to complete a story, and can identify a market for that work, then once it is professionally edited, start submitting for publication. If you still can't get a publisher, investigate one or more of the many avenues available today to get your work in front of your audience!*

ENJOY!

INTRODUCTION

"From an Idea...to your Finished Story," as narrated by "The Three Wise Writing Guides," is an interactive journey into the exciting world of writing. On this journey our guides: **the Writer**, Ms. Iwanna B. Writer, **the Editor**, Ms. Edi Tor, and **the Publisher**, Mr. I.M. Publisher, will give tips, information and interactive writing tools designed to help anyone who wants to write. This combined text/workbook was developed as a direct result of the authors' years of experience, as published authors, editors and publishers. From our writing workshops and interactive seminars we gained an understanding of writers' specific needs. We concluded, that most participants were unable to take their ideas from the seedling stage to the finished story. For the most part, great story ideas would pop-up, then ultimately fizzle, from the task of getting these ideas down on paper. Workshop questionnaires and writing assignments revealed that not only aspiring writers, but also the more experienced, could benefit from learning how to properly structure their great ideas into finished stories. Overcoming obstacles by setting realistic goals proved to be helpful in keeping writers on track and motivating them to complete their projects. Once they began to think like writers, the quality of their work improved and they were able to see their writing projects through to completion.

How Will This Book Benefit You?

Whether you're a beginner or an established writer, *"HOW TO WRITE YOUR BOOK From an Idea...to YOUR PUBLISHED STORY,"* was designed to meet any writer's needs. Our Three Writing Guides will assist you through the process: prepare you to write, help you get your good ideas down on paper and walk you through revising and editing. They'll stay with you as you finish your work and prepare your manuscript, and then offer advice to those of you with an eye toward publishing. Different people write for different reasons. Whether your reasons are profit, therapy or to see your ideas down on paper, or in print, they want to HELP YOU!

HOW TO WRITE YOUR BOOK From an Idea to YOUR PUBLISHED STORY   INTRODUCTION

So, is this book is right for you?

Take this quiz:

- You've ever envisioned writing a book, but didn't know where to start — so you didn't start.

- You've ever sat down to write and got stalled — so you never continued.

- You've ever written your ideas down on paper, but couldn't turn them into a story.

- You've ever finished a writing project, and then didn't know what to do with it.

- You've ever finished your writing project and had friends tell you it would be the next best seller, but it wasn't.

- You've ever sent your work to publishers and received rejections.

- You've received rejections that upset you, and eventually stopped sending out your work.

- You've put your work in a bottom drawer; believing you would take it out someday— but you didn't.

If you were nodding, "...that's happened to me," then Today is YOUR Writer's Birthday and the Wise Guides have a SPECIAL Gift for You... **This Book!**

Understanding your writing needs, the authors have chosen the Three Wise Writing Guides to travel with you on your writing journey.

Our Guides will:

- pinpoint important information to help you map out your voyage

- highlight details to be aware of to ensure a completed journey

- give you writing assignments to help you perfect your skills and enable you to maneuver around the bumps in the road

- provide helpful hints, and detours to take when you hit writer's roadblocks

- urge you on with a suitcase packed full of helpful resources

The Wise Guides will provide you with maps you'll need to travel to your writing destination and ensure that you have a safe, completed journey. Best of all they will be your Passenger and Navigator as you Journey together —*"...From an Idea to YOUR PUBLISHED STORY."*

This book is designed to be instructional and interactive. To get the most out of your trip, use the examples you'll find throughout the book to give you a better understanding of the writing topics. The Travel Kit forms, found at the back of each chapter, will reinforce the information in that chapter and give you an opportunity to develop your story. You will also be prompted to "DO IT NOW" at various points on your journey. We suggest you use these areas to personalize your writing. If you've already written your story, then you can use all of these points for editing and revising. Whether you're a novice or an experienced writer, this book has been designed to provide a step-by-step approach to writing and completing your story. Our guides were designed from what we've learned about writing and as a way to make this a fun experience that will spur you on to travel **"...*to YOUR PUBLISHED STORY.*"**

Look for Road Signs to Help You on Your Journey

These signs have been designed to ensure you don't get lost. They'll keep you pointed in the right direction and on the right roads during every aspect of your writing trip.

HOW TO WRITE YOUR BOOK From an Idea to YOUR PUBLISHED STORY   INTRODUCTION

Writing Map 1 **Trip Signs:** These Writing Map Signs will identify each new chapter of your journey as a color coordinated Writing Map. Think of these signs as the Welcome Sign you see when entering a new state that you must pass through to get to your final destination. Each sign will also correspond to the forms you'll need that are located in your Travel Kit at the back of each chapter.

DO IT NOW! **Map Sign:** This sign will alert you to STOP and Do whatever assignment is suggested. Doing these assignments at the time will help to reinforce the information.

Travel Folders: Throughout this book you'll be prompted to create folders. We suggest setting up physical File Folders as well as computer files. Your Travel Kit of Forms are at the end of each Chapter. The Forms are divided into example and exercise. The examples all follow our own action packed story "Code 47 to BREV Force."

Suitcase: Finally we have to pack for the voyage— So use this SUITCASE to Pack all materials, supplies, file folders, forms and any other materials you will need to travel, *...to YOUR PUBLISHED STORY."* Each chapter review will tell you what to put in your suitcase. Remember Your Suitcase is also our organizer file. It should contain everything you'll need and can be a physical file and a computer file.

Pit Stops: This book also offers interactive Service Stations placed strategically along your route to assist you in making those necessary pit stops such as Web Support — E-mail Tech Support — and Benefits all designed to help you get back on the road. Look for these Road Signs when you need that pit stop!

We also suggest that whenever you want to remember some point we've made — use a highlighter. If we trigger something specific that you want to remember when you begin writing your story — use **RED** on that page or in the margin next to the information. Devise your own personal method for using this book to get you started on your voyage.

Writing is hard work— but anything worthwhile is worth working for. But also remember that writing is an art that can be learned; it's not brain surgery. No matter what level of writing skills you possess, by following the techniques laid out in this book, you should be able to see yourself as a writer and achieve your goal of a completed manuscript. We also want you to remember — books can be written in a matter of months— or a matter of years. Some authors take years because they write and then put their work in a drawer for stretches of time. We imagine more good books are in drawers, then have been published. If this describes you, go get your work now and take it out — if you haven't started; commit with us now to get started!

Think of your writing as embarking on an adventure, and sticking with it until you reach your writing destination. If you do, you'll have a more positive outlook, and a stronger motivation to finish your work.

It takes confidence and belief in what you're trying to accomplish in order to begin this journey. The Three Wise Writing Guides believe in you; after all, you've taken the first step by using, *"HOW TO WRITE YOUR BOOK From an Idea...to YOUR PUBLISHED STORY,"* to help you get started with your writing. They'll lead you on the right roads and provide the knowledge and tools you'll need for a successful trip. The Guides will be with you every step, until your journey is completed. Ask any writer what an accomplishment it is to finish a work and believe you've done everything to make it the best.

Success doesn't necessarily happen overnight. Writing journeys can be filled with unexpected delays, road blocks, detours and pitfalls. Just believe that when you finally reach your destination and have a finished work—it will all have been worthwhile! So let's get the right vehicle, pack everything you need, including your travel Maps, and follow The Three Writing Guides down the Golden Quill Roads to Your Finished, Published Story!

BON VOYAGE!!!

PLAN YOUR WRITING JOURNEY

Before you begin any journey you must plan:

- Where you want to go
- How you will get there
- What you need to pack
- What you will do when you get there etc.

And, like any great trip, having an experienced guide can help you avoid the bumps in the road and make the experience that much better. Ms.Iwanna B. Writer will be assisting you through this phase of your writing trip. Ms. Edi Tor and Mr. I.M. Publisher will also add their comments throughout this stage.

Planning List: Set Your Writing Destination.

Have you ever wondered what would've happened if Christopher Columbus or other explorers had started their journey without a defined destination? Have you ever wondered why so many people who have started on journey's into the unknown, braved hardships and never gave up? They believed in their dreams; addressed potential obstacles, anticipated achieving their goals and then off they went--confident of their destination.

Our Guide's Agree and Suggest

 Take your great ideas, unfinished works, or writing that you have stashed in a drawer; and let's get started NOW!

First, set your writing destination:

    Are you writing for?

- ❑ Yourself
- ❑ Others
- ❑ To Publish

    I want to begin my writing journey with a

- ❑ Book
- ❑ Short Story/Article
- ❑ Personal History
- ❑ Other_____

Once you can identify your destination clearly, your next step will be: to get organized, prepare the right tools and establish a designated place to write. Then, you will need to plan a convenient time to write.

 Use this checklist to get started:

◆ **You Need A Place To Write** This doesn't have to be a mountain top retreat, or a penthouse suite. Many of our best writers have produced their most outstanding work under less than ideal circumstances. Some started writing: in a basement, garage, on the kitchen table, park bench or any place they could use pen and paper. Do you have a place to write? If not, you need to find one. It should be secure, quiet and private.

- ❑ Decide on a location where you will write.
- ❑ Make a "DO NOT DISTURB" sign to put on the door.
- ❑ Set up your files and supplies.
- ❑ **Most Importantly** — Don't forget to tell your family!

It's very important in achieving your goals that your family understand your commitment and extend their complete support.

◆ **You Need to Choose Your Vehicle For Writing: Computer, Typewriter,(some still use a typewriter), Tape Recorder, Dictation or Longhand or any method you choose**

Some of our best literature was, and still is, written in longhand or on clattering typewriters. But in this day and age, if you can use a computer, that might be the vehicle of choice. Computers make it much easier to write, revise and save your work. They can also give you access to the internet for unlimited research and resources. If you've been thinking about a computer, consider it an investment in your writing future. It's important to have an easy-to-use and up-to-date version of a word processing software. Microsoft Word is currently popular for PC's (personal computers) and is considered fairly easy to use. If you do choose a computer our experts want you to remember these important rules that will save you time, aggravation and the possibility of lost work — Be sure to have some type of back-up system, either thumb drives or any external back-up system: clouds provide good protection! **Save** the entire work to that system. Also while you're writing, Always, Always **SAVE OFTEN! And Be Sure-** Whenever you finish a writing time Save Again!

If you're going to require lessons to use computer software – it may be too complicated and delay your leaving on your writing journey. So, find the vehicle that best suits your needs or, go back to what has worked for published authors in the past — typewriters or just plain longhand! Remember you can always get your writing computerized later. Time is money and timely topics burn hot and then fizzle out. Don't wait until you are computer savvy to get started writing.

HOW TO WRITE YOUR BOOK   From an Idea to YOUR PUBLISHED STORY   Plan Your Writing Journey

◆ **You Need the Right Writing Tools**. Keeping pads, pens and sharpened pencils around the house, an tablet or cell phone, especially by your bed for those late night ideas, works great! Small notebooks in your purse or jacket and post-its in your house, office and car can be a big help for jotting down ideas that come when you least expect them. When placing your post-it's around be sure the family and or co-workers know they're only intended for your writing notes. Don't forget to put those notes in your Travel Folder (see below). And, because you never know when you'll get a flash of inspiration driving in the car, or taking long walks, use your phone or a small tape recorder as a great way to capture your ideas. Don't forget a good dictionary and thesaurus are also essential writing tools. Sometimes just changing that one word to something more descriptive can greatly enhance your work.

◆ **You Need to Set Up Your Travel Folders**. Set up a system of 8½" x 11" file folders (different colors can make this an easy information access system), in which you pack all your ideas, notes and research information. Separate folders keep your work organized and help you sort ideas. These folders should be easily accessible in your writing area. Make it a habit of putting a date on your notes and review the newest ones before each new writing   session.   If you're using a computer, set up a main folder for your work on your desktop and then create sub-folders for your computer notes within that folder. Example: "...HOW TO WRITE YOUR BOOK ," is the main folder. Then inside that folder is your main manuscript and sub-folders for your notes. If you do use computer folders we suggest in addition to those folders you also have a few manila file folders, (as described above), just to organized and notes you may generate .

Now that we have everything for your trip the next step is to PACK!

Our Guides Packing List :
Once you've gathered everything on your list, set up your writing area so that it's comfortable and ready for you to begin your writing session.

Get your Writing Map 1 **PACKING LIST** Form
from your Travel Kit at the back of this chapter

Fill in your writing supplies
When Completed store in your Travel Folder

Questions: info@goldenquillpress.com Subject line HTWYB–Map 1

◆ **You Need Time to Write**. It would be ideal to be able to write full time, but many writers don't have that luxury. Try to work out your schedule; your job and family – to find the time you need. As we've suggested, having family support can play a big role in achieving your writing destination.

Managing your writing time is also taking control of your life. Twenty-four hours seems like a lot of time to some people; little time to others.   It's all a matter of how you manage your activities and how you view priorities. The Three Wise Guides use the motto: **"Save time by ditching the clutter."**   Have on hand only the items you need. Have a place for everything and everything in its place.

Try to analyze your day and see where you have time-wasting activities**.** Keep a record of what you do each day for an entire week to help you see where your time is spent. When your daily schedule involves a number of activities, you will need to find the best time to write: Many daily activities can't be changed, but if you really want

HOW TO WRITE YOUR BOOK   From an Idea to YOUR PUBLISHED STORY   Plan Your Writing Journey

time to write, you must find the time— and you will! It's not so much a matter of when you write, but that you write as often and as much as possible. One of the main reasons is to help you retain your continuity of thought. If you do not have a structured writing schedule the task of continuing thoughts from previous writing sessions will be much more difficult.

The WRITING APPOINTMENT CALENDAR in the back of this chapter will help you set the best times for writing. There's a saying: "If you don't know where you're going, that's where you'll go—nowhere," so, use this Calendar to follow your course and keep you on the right writing track to finishing your work. Remember: *If you search for it—you will find it,* and in this case time is of the essence. Congratulate yourself when you find extra time and feel good about that writing session time (If you feel guilty, it will show in your work—so, just find another time). Plan your writing time, the same way you make any important commitment, except this one, is with yourself. You wouldn't cancel an appointment that's important to your future, so be sure to adhere to these times. Look at your schedule today and commit to a regular time to write. Start with small steps you can handle; even if it's just a brief amount of time. Writing at regular intervals is more important at first than how long each session lasts. Once you get started you'll find the time to write on a regular basis.

Most of us have the best intentions -- I will go to the gym today, I will take a walk-- I will write-- but most times if we don't set that time aside, the end of the day comes and you're amazed that you didn't get any of these things done. We've learned from our writing seminars that when life happens, writing time can be the first to go. But, when we had our writers establish set times and prioritize their activities, they succeeded in not only finding the time, but becoming disciplined enough to make the time.

Writers generally think they can create the perfect story in less time than it took to create the world. We must think realistically and plan to write regularly!

Set that appointment and don't forget to mark it in your daily planner or wherever you keep track of appointments.
Tell family, work associates and friends, so they don't schedule Something during your writing time!

Get your Writing Map 1 **APPOINTMENT CALENDAR** Form
from your Travel Kit at the back of this chapter.

Fill out the information as shown in the example on the next page
When Completed store in your Travel Folder

Questions: info@goldenquillpress.com Subject line HTWYB–Map 1

Then, use the Appointment Calendar and mark every time you have a writing session, how long it lasted and what you accomplished.
Post it prominently, where it will be visible to you, daily.

HOW TO WRITE YOUR BOOK   From an Idea to YOUR PUBLISHED STORY   Plan Your Writing Journey

Don't Forget to go over all your Actual Writing Times at the end of each week to review your accomplishments and use the information as a guide to set your schedule for the following week. Then, put the finished form in Your Writing Appointments Folder for future reference.

Monday	Time		Appointment Assignment	Time		Actually Completed
	From	To	*Work On Main Character*	From	To	*Completed Main Character &*
June 5 / 06	*7:30 PM*	*11:00 PM*	*Development* **EXAMPLE**	*8:00 PM*	*10:30 PM*	*Her Family - 5 Characters -* *Put in File*

◆ **You Need to Set Priorities**. Creative writers often have many good ideas, but don't take time to sort them out. Sometimes those ideas are like a traveler without a map or a tapestry with threads going in all directions. Being disciplined helps you to focus on the big picture—your finished work. It's best to concentrate on only one writing project now and give yourself a reasonable deadline. Procrastination is the writer's greatest enemy! If you set positive and realistic goals, you will have a better chance of succeeding.   Decide what you want to accomplish first; then begin working toward completing that writing project.

In order to keep you on track we recommend establishing an anticipated completion date and writing that date at the bottom of each of your Appointment Calendars. Use that date to review your accomplishments and to try and set a realistic completion date.

 Make a sign to display in your writing space to remind you of the goal you are working toward!

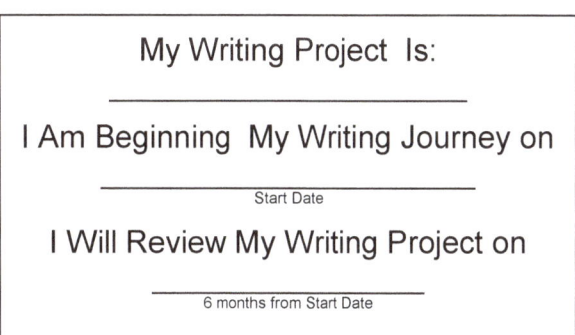

◆   **You Need to Have Purpose**. Why do you want to write? This is a question only you can answer.

The following list was compiled from a questionnaire used in a writer's workshop that asked writers of various ages, occupations and lifestyles: "Why do you want to write?" Their answers may help you gain more insight into your own reasons for writing.

Check off the answers that most closely express your reasons.
I want to write because:

- ❑ I have a passion for reading good literature and writing gives me an opportunity to see my ideas come alive on the page.
- ❑ I find writing helps me to express my inner feelings about life and the world around me.
- ❑ I have a story I feel needs to be told and I am strongly motivated to write.
- ❑ Writing is my life. I find it therapeutic.
- ❑ I believe everyone has a story to tell and I'd like to write my story.
- ❑ I would like to become a published author. Not so much for fame or fortune (though that would be nice), but to share my knowledge and experiences with others.
- ❑ I want to become a published author for the money and fame.
- ❑ Writing is a creative activity I enjoy.
- ❑ Writing well is an asset in my career. Companies today are looking for applicants that have good communication skills. Writing skills top the list.

Take a moment, sit back and think; then add your "Travel Statement" to Our list.
I want to write because

_____

_____

 SHARE your reasons for writing
Your comments will be posted online:

e-mail to: info@goldenquillpress.com
Subject line: Comments—Reasons for Writing

Now that we understand why you want to write let's see what skills you have and what you need to work on.

◆ **You Need to Chart Your Strengths and Weaknesses**
The purpose of the chart that follows is to identify your strongest skills and positive personal qualities you can use to accomplish your task of finishing the work you start. In every workshop we've, conducted procrastination was the one problem most writers agreed they needed to overcome. They got started okay, but then let everything else get in the way. Understanding this road block in advance will help you when "life happens." Remember too, that sometimes it's easier to put your writing away than it is to work through a problem. So you need to be prepared.

◆ **You need to use the chart to develop better skills**.
Writing is an art and craft that is easy for some and difficult for others. Use the chart to increase your Positive traits. Remember: "Patience, Practice and Persistence.! This Chart will help you Use Your Positive Points to Overcome your Negative Ones and to plan a course of action when something happens to interfere with your writing!

HOW TO WRITE YOUR BOOK   From an Idea to YOUR PUBLISHED STORY   Plan Your Writing Journey

Personal Evaluation Chart

List + STRONG POINTS qualities, skills and accomplishments	List – WEAK POINTS obstacles to overcome to reach writing goals

Use the list above to help yourself --

Example: If you were discouraged because of a writer's block and decided to stop writing (Negative Trait) Your (Positive) Strong Determination and commitment would see you through!

HOW TO WRITE YOUR BOOK   From an Idea to YOUR PUBLISHED STORY   Plan Your Writing Journey

TRIP REVIEW

Map Directions

Every Successful Journey Begins With A Plan

Writers Succeed One Mile At A Time

Sticking To Road Maps Will Get You To Your Final Destination

New Roads Can Offer New Ideas

Travel Instructions — Did You?

- ❏ Stake out your Place to Write & discuss with your family
- ❏ Obtain Tools and Equipment for your writing needs
- ❏ Make Time to Write
- ❏ Design a Writing Appointments Schedule to help keep track of your writing times, post it prominently where you will see it often
- ❏ Decide on an anticipated completion Date

OUR WISE GUIDES
POINT YOU IN THE RIGHT DIRECTION

Being well prepared will help you to stay on track!

Get used to using a Dictionary and a Thesaurus. They are wonderful tools!

CONGRATUATIONS!! We are all 100% behind your efforts!

◀ **NOTE** ▶
New technologies are constantly presenting exciting challenges for writers. Even when you feel confident of your writing abilities, it's always important to keep your eye on ways to improve your skills and present the best finished product possible.
Reading published authors will help you develop better skills.

Start Date: _____   Anticipated Completion Date: _____

HOW TO WRITE YOUR BOOK   From an Idea to YOUR PUBLISHED STORY   Plan Your Writing Journey

Writing Map 1   WRITING APPOINTMENT CALENDAR

Monday	Time From	To	Appointment Assignment	Time From	To	Actually Completed
June 5 / 06	7:30 PM	11:00 PM	*Work On Main Character Development* **EXAMPLE**	8:00 PM	10:30 PM	*Completed Main Character & Her Family – 5 Characters – Put in File*

WRITING APPOINTMENT CALENDAR   W/E _____

	Time From	To	Appointment Assignment	Time From	To	Actually Completed
Sunday						
Monday						
Tuesday						
Wednesday						
Thursday						
Friday						
Saturday						

Go Over all your Actual Writing Sessions at the end of the week to review your writing times and use the information as a guide to set your schedule for the following week. Then put this form in Your Writing Appointments Folder for future reference.

HOW TO WRITE YOUR BOOK   From an Idea to YOUR PUBLISHED STORY   Plan Your Writing Journey

Writing Map 1 — YOUR PACKING LIST — Travel Kit Form

The Guides Packing List :

- ☐ Pens (Include a RED Pen & Highlighters)
- ☐ Post-it's (Get a STAND OUT Color or Florescent, but not too dark so you can't read what you write   BRIGHT YELLOW may work)
- ☐ Manila Folders (Colors are preferable)
- ☐ 8.5 11 White Paper
- ☐ Small Tape Recorder &Tapes—Phone /Tablet
- ☐ Computer Travel Drives / CD's (depending upon your system needs)

- ☐ Pencils with Erasers
- ☐ Pencil Sharpener
- ☐ Pads
- ☐ Notebook
- ☐ Dictionary
- ☐ Thesaurus
- ☐ Timer
- ☐ Do Not Disturb Sign
- ☐ Your Writing Goal Sign

OTHER: _____   _____   _____

- ♦ _____   _____   _____
- ♦ _____   _____   _____
- ♦ _____   _____   _____
- ♦ _____   _____   _____
- ♦ _____   _____   _____
- ♦ _____   _____   _____
- ♦ _____   _____   _____
- ♦ _____   _____   _____
- ♦ _____   _____   _____
- ♦ _____   _____   _____

HOW TO WRITE YOUR BOOK   From an Idea to YOUR PUBLISHED STORY   Preparing To Write

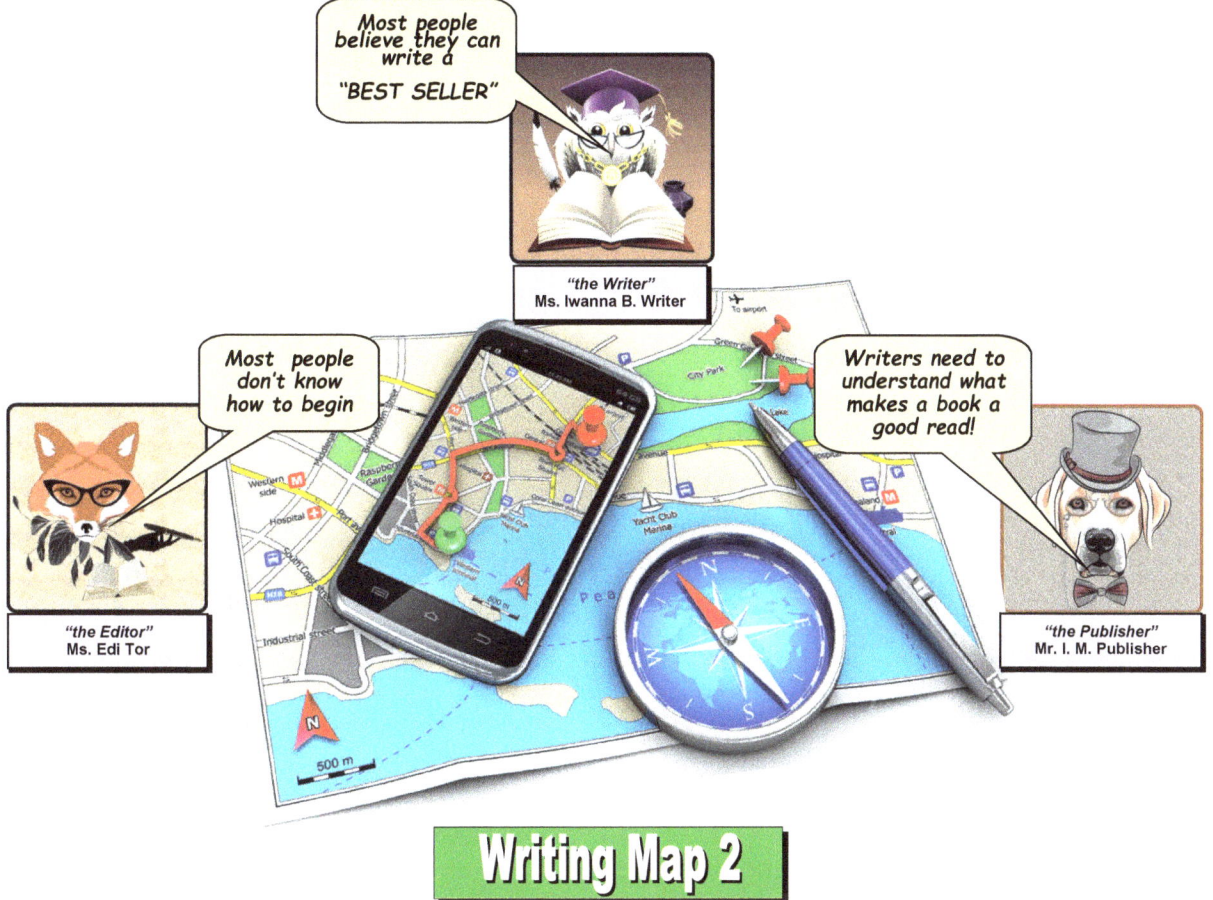

PREPARING TO WRITE

Now that we've settled on a place to write and have gotten all necessary materials gathered into our writing suitcase, it's time to begin formulating story ideas. Whether you're writing a short story, or a novel, the process is essentially the same. You need to begin at the beginning with an idea. Writer's sometimes want to start with a Title and they spend a great deal of time and effort deciding on one. But, as you will learn, titles can change, so don't be too concerned with the Title now! Just choose a temporary title that you feel comfortable with.

How do you begin to gather your story ideas. Ideas for stories generally are derived from personal experiences. Many people want to write about their own life or a loved one. Some people write strictly from imagination; building a concept then expanding on it. Others get ideas from: headlines, reading about places and events, but where ever your ideas come from, you need to have a clear understanding of your idea before you begin writing. In Writing Map 1 you began your writing journey, now let's continue down the road to getting you, "*...From an Idea to YOUR PUBLISHED STORY.*"

The best way to do that is to ask a lot of questions—

My Writing Idea is about:

❏ My Life
❏ Someone Else's Life

❏ A Story I will conceive

❏ History : People, Places or Events

❏ Other_____

(real or conceived)

Decide whether Your Story is Fiction Or Non - Fiction

Fiction: invented, imaginary stories, made up by the author not restricted to fact

Non-Fiction: stories based on fact, rather than the imagination
My Story is   ❏ Fiction   ❏ Non-Fiction

Decide On A Format

Format is the writing plan for constructing your story that applies to a short story, novella or a novel.

Short story: shorter than a novel, normally dealing with fewer characters and less action – generally between 7,000 and 10,000 words, but can be fewer. Science Fiction is generally less than 7,500 words.

Novella: a short novel, more than 7,500 but fewer than 40,000 words.

Novel: much longer than the short story, generally, 40,000 words or more. This format enables the writer to develop a wider range of characters and a much more complex plot.
My Format is   ❏ Short Story   ❏ Novella   ❏ Novel

Mapping out a Premise

The premise of a story is a statement or assertion on which your story is based and is the seed from which your story will grow. So how do you decide on your premise. Think of your premise as a descriptive explanation of your idea. Instead of saying, I'm writing about my life, say, I'm writing about being an American growing up in Europe during World War II. So you see, we've expanded the idea just by embellishing the statement.

Get your Writing Map 2 **IDEA TO OUTLINE** Form
from your Travel Kit at the back of this chapter

Fill out the information on #1 and #2 IDEA / PREMISE
When Completed store in your Travel Folder

Questions: info@goldenquillpress.com Subject line HTWYB–Map 2

The Five "W's" Structuring Formula

As any reporter will tell you there's a formula for writing an outline for a good story and we suggest using the same formula for your writing. When structuring a story, the five "W's" formula can help you keep organized.

The five "W's" are:

- Who -   Who is the story about?

- What -   What happened?

- Where - Where did it happen?

- When - When did it happen?

- Why -   Why did it happen?

- **Note:**   How did it happen? *(we also add How)

Whether you're a beginning novelist or an experienced writer, the five "W's" formula is especially helpful to any writer as a structuring guide. The "W's" need not be in the order shown here, but a well told story needs to include each point.

Get your Writing Map 2 **IDEA TO OUTLINE** Form
from your Travel Kit at the back of this chapter

Add #3 - the 5W's that pertain to your story
When Completed store in your Travel Folder

Questions: info@goldenquillpress.com Subject line HTWYB–Map 2

The Outline Highway

One of the best ways to plan a story is to take your premise and your 5 W's and make a list or outline of the most important points you want to cover. An outline helps you to see your story take shape. You might think it's easier to just sit down at the computer or with a pen and blank paper and let your story flow.

But your Writer and Editor guides suggest:

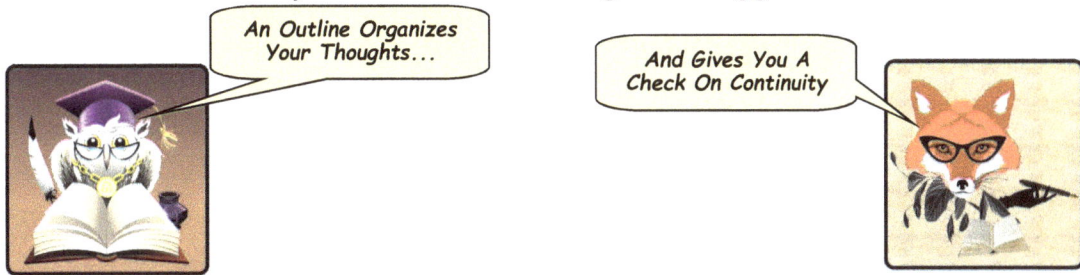

An outline will help you organize your story and keep an accurate flow, while helping you tie up loose ends. A good outline makes your story come full circle with a beginning, a middle and an end.

Think of the outline as the skeleton of a story (the basic or rough concept) which you then add flesh to with additional details. In our workshops we demonstrate "fleshing" by drawing a skeleton. Then as we add details to the story, such as plot, characters, settings, time periods and much more, the flesh is added as it takes shape over the bones.

REMEMBER This basic working outline helps you to get a clear picture of how to get *"from your idea to your finished story."*

EXAMPLE:

#1 IDEA: Adventurers of a lost Bear.

#2 PREMISE: A priceless bear is missing from the zoo.

#3 THE 5W's:

Who - A priceless white bear cub named Polar

2nd Who - Dr. John Kay, director of the Zoo   **Note**: stories can have many who's for one subject so try and answer the pertinent Who's first

What – Polar the Bear Cub was reported stolen from the Zoo, but was later reported wandering around Ellisville

Where - Ellisville Park Zoo

When - 5 a.m. Tuesday, May 15

Why - An investigation is underway. Police Chief Bill Norton said bear knapping had not been ruled out, because the bear is an endangered species and is priceless

How – The door was found open

HOW TO WRITE YOUR BOOK   From an Idea to YOUR PUBLISHED STORY   Preparing To Write

#4 OUTLINE:.

Dr. John Kay, director of the Ellisville Park Zoo, reported that a bear named Polar; a priceless cub, listed on the endangered species list, had disappeared from the zoo early Tuesday morning. The bear's attendant found the door of the steel-wire cage open and officials couldn't rule out bear-knapping. When questioned the zoo attendant, however, swore he didn't leave the door unlatched. Later reports stated the bear was wandering on the highway north of Ellisville, without the so called, "knapper." The bear was eventually found at the "Old Honey Mill," and was returned to the zoo unharmed. Police Chief, Bill Norton said officials told him Polar, now weighed considerably more than when he went AWOL. Everyone concluded the bear had a fine time. A last minute note to this story stated that the Honey Mill has submitted a bill to the zoo for $900.00, as the mill was left totally devoid of any honey after Polar's visit.

This basic outline can now be expanded as you add more details

If you have any questions about outlining, you can e-mail tech support at:
info@goldenquillpress.com Subject—Outlining—with your questions

 Get your Writing Map 2 **IDEA TO OUTLINE** Form
from your Travel Kit at the back of this chapter

Add #4 - your OUTLINE to your form
When Completed store in your Travel Folder

Questions: info@goldenquillpress.com Subject line HTWYB–Map 2

HOW TO WRITE YOUR BOOK   From an Idea to YOUR PUBLISHED STORY   Preparing To Write

TRIP REVIEW

Map Directions

A Good Premise Is A Write Sturdy Foundation

5 W's Formula Help You Get From Who To Where & When To How

Cover Your Skeleton By Fleshing Out The Details

Non-Fiction Or Fiction - Different As Driving On City Streets Or Taking The Highway

Travel Instructions — Did You?

- ❏ Fill in your Road Sign: Ideas, Fiction or Non-Fiction, Format
- ❏ Decide on your Premise
- ❏ Go over the 5 W's for your story
- ❏ Write your Basic Outline
- ❏ Now put the form in your Ideas File in your

OUR WISE GUIDES
POINT YOU IN THE RIGHT DIRECTION

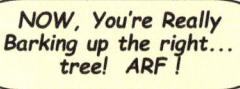

◀ **NOTE** ▶

You can turn your ideas into a great story by staying on track and letting your premise drive your outline.

HOW TO WRITE YOUR BOOK   From an Idea to YOUR PUBLISHED STORY   Preparing To Write

Writing Map 2 — FROM IDEA TO OUTLINE — Travel Kit Form

EXAMPLE:

#1 IDEA: Imagined Computer Virus/Super Heroes

#2 PREMISE: Computer Virus goes beyond it's programming

#3 THE 5W's:

Who - Controller-computer virus gone awry

2ⁿᵈ Who - Cracko– hologram **Note**: stories can have many who's for one subject so try and answer the pertinent Who's first

What – Controller uses Cracko to recruit college students

Where - Island Falls

When - An unknown time

Why - To become the strongest entity in the world

How – By invading all systems and recruiting a human army

#4 OUTLINE:.

A computer virus has grown beyond its original programming and has invaded the small college town of Island Falls. Controller has programmed holograms to do its bidding and to persuade college students to join its ranks.

Scientists Martin and Vivian Kane are recruited to stop Controller. Their children's (Brad and Evie) best friend Jonathan becomes hooked by Controller's forces (hologram Cracko and human helper Sheila) and Brad and Evie strike out on their own to defeat Controller.

YOUR OUTLINE:

#1 IDEA: _____

#2 PREMISE: _____
_____

#3 THE 5W's:

Who - _____

2ⁿᵈ Who - _____
_____
_____
_____

What – _____
_____
_____

Where - _____

When - _____

Why - _____
_____

How - _____

#4 OUTLINE: _____
_____
_____
_____
_____
_____
_____
_____
_____
_____
_____
_____
_____
_____
_____
_____

Writing Map 3

FLESHING OUT YOUR STORY

Just as an architect has a blueprint; a pilot, a flight plan and a cook, a recipe, you need to organize all the major points of your story before you begin to write. These techniques will also help you stay on track throughout your story.

Bringing Your Characters to Life

When you read a story in a newspaper, magazine or book, it generally centers on people. Usually it isn't about a house, but the people who live there. So, your story must create characters who come to life for your readers. Characters need to make an impression or your story will fall flat. Think of some of the simple adventure stories for children, from "Beauty and the Beast" to "The Three Little Pigs, or Goldilocks." It's easy to remember these characters because even in their simplicity, they are vibrant and almost jump off the page with life. In our creative writing workshops, beginning writers often ask, "Just how can I breathe life into my characters?" A good place to begin is to choose your main character, who is called the protagonist: the principal character of a story. This character can be the good guy, someone who champions a cause, but keep in mind, the protagonist doesn't have to be the hero.

HOW TO WRITE YOUR BOOK   From an Idea to YOUR PUBLISHED STORY   Fleshing Out Your Story

On the other hand the antagonist, often the bad guy, opposes the protagonist, (main character). He or she might be an open enemy, rival, or the character that creates obstacles to be overcome. Your job is to make your characters believable and unforgettable.

Get your Writing Map 2 **Idea to Outline** Form from your Travel Kit . Look at "WHO," this is your

Main Character the one the majority of the story revolves around

Questions: info@goldenquillpress.com Subject line HTWYB–Map 3

My Main Character Is_____

Now let's FLESH out that character!

Go sit on a park bench, on a bus, stand in an aisle in the grocery store or anyplace where you can observe total strangers. Now find someone who looks right for your main character. Imagine that person playing your character in your story — Is he or she a good fit ? If not, try again until you find your perfect main character. Observing people is the best method for character development.

Once you've gotten a good picture of what your character should look like, you can give that character and appropriate name. **Our Experts Suggest:** The Name Game

Naming your Characters

All names have meaning and a writer has thousands of names to choose from when building characters

You can also visit your local library or book store to find a name book. An internet search for boys names or girls names will also return numerous sites of interest.

Names used in historical novels, such as Heathcliff, Esmeralda or other dated writings require more research. Names that are popular today may not have been around in the past. However, some names, especially from biblical times, never seem to go out of date. It's up to the author to choose appropriate names while keeping the reader in mind. Names that are totally wrong for the character only detract from the writer's credibility.

HOW TO WRITE YOUR BOOK   From an Idea to YOUR PUBLISHED STORY   Fleshing Out Your Story

NAMES Should Be Memorable! Like Heathcliff!

Last Names can have as much impact as First Names. They tell a great deal about the character's origin's: Scarlet O'Hara, Obi Wan Kenobi. When you add a last name it can bring your character a whole new dimension: When naming characters, try to choose names that fit without obvious stereotyping. Don't give a serious character a silly name.

Sure, or RHETT, SCARLETT, MICKEY MOUSE! How 'Bout Harry Potter?

 Take Time To Choose the Right Name for your Main Character

Character Identity Crisis

When you begin to examine people, you'll find that real people aren't perfect. You want your characters to hold a fascination for the reader, whether they're a good character or a bad one. If they're perfect they may not be believable or interesting. Now try to study people you know. What are their personality traits? What habits do they have? What qualities distinguish them?   Find their good and bad sides-- Now think of your main character and imagine that character's good traits and bad.

Without Faults and Imperfections characters will look like Naked Skeletons

In our workshops, participants have told us it's often difficult to remember everything about their characters, especially when they have more than one or two interacting in a story.

Remember you're your character's creator and in order to write believable characters you need to have a clear picture of all of your character's details. Detailing is a way for you to not only get a very clear picture of your characters, but also a way to keep all the information about those characters straight.

Get your Writing Map 3 **CHARACTER DETAILING** Form
from your Travel Kit at the back of this chapter.

Decide on one Main Character Fill in all information - Repeat for others
When Completed store in your Travel Folder

Questions: info@goldenquillpress.com Subject line HTWYB–Map 3

We suggest you take a great deal of time and really "flesh" out this part of your   skeleton. The more you do now the easier it will be when you begin to write. Refer to your Travel Kit Forms often to remind you to use the character's physical, mental and emotional makeup and to help you keep your facts about them straight.

Additional Tips

In our workshops, we learned that some writers have expressed a need for even more visual representation of their characters. We suggest you take paper, pencil and crayons and draw figures of each of your characters and then fill in the details. You don't have to be an artist—stick figures will do. Be sure to approximate size and height and fill in the color of his or her hair, eyes and other details. Some writers also build a file of interesting looking people they find in photos or in magazines to help them achieve a more visual concept of someone they want their characters to resemble.

Sometimes minor characters are written in to help move the story along. If you barely mention someone in a scene, then you should write only the necessary details. For instance, if your lead character, a Detective Sam Sharp, stops at a hot dog stand and says: "Hi Joe. How's business. Gimme one with mustard and a coke." Unless Joe has a part in the story, that can be all the reader needs to know. But suppose Joe is an undercover police officer and the hot dog stand has been set up as a front. Now we have a reason for Detective Sam to stop by the hot dog stand and we need more information about Joe..

It's important to have a reason for people, places or things in a scene, but superfluous details bog down your story and bore the reader. Props can be used effectively to help flesh out your character, but they must have a purpose. If Detective Sam stands by the hot dog stand, he must have a reason. He may sip coffee, or tie his shoe—all the while exchanging information with Joe, but to anyone who might be watching, the scene would appear to be no more than two men discussing a hot dog.

Send your Character to the Casting Director

Before you begin writing, you should be sure you've created characters who will be memorable. Think of your favorite movie—and then imagine the main character as someone very different – usually it doesn't work. Now think of a character from your favorite book. Can you close your eyes and picture not only what that character looks like, but the way the character acts and speaks. Sometimes even the most insignificant character leaves a lasting impression, so don't skimp on detailing all your important characters.

The best way to check if you have created viable characters is to Go back to your **Map# 3 Character Detailing Form.** Look over the details of the main character in your story and then ask yourself whether or not a casting director could take your **Character Detailing Form** and know exactly which actor or actress should play that character in the movie.

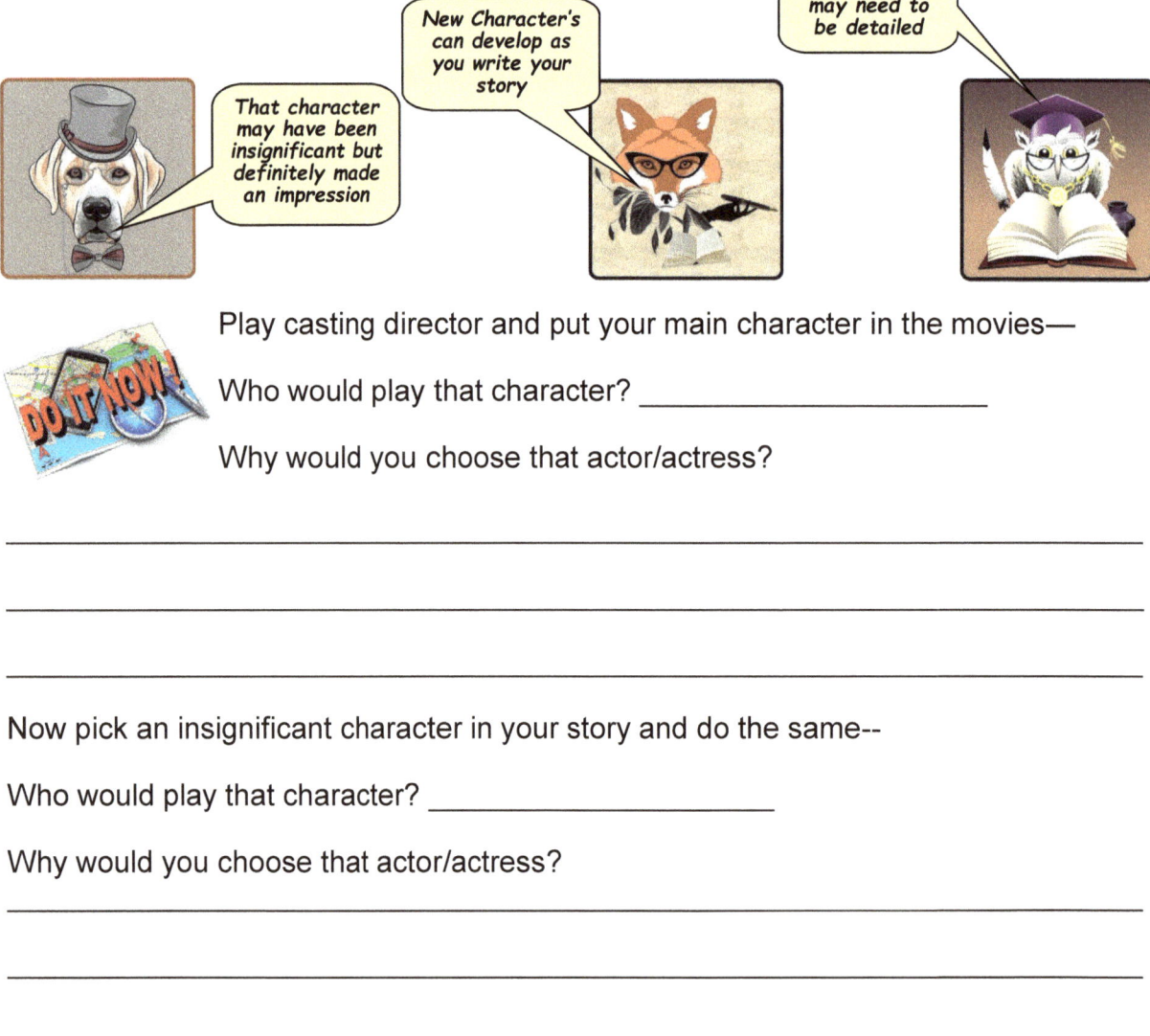

Play casting director and put your main character in the movies—

Who would play that character? _____

Why would you choose that actor/actress?

_____
_____
_____

Now pick an insignificant character in your story and do the same--

Who would play that character? _____

Why would you choose that actor/actress?
_____
_____
_____

Take a lesson from the producer of "Gone With The Wind," David O. Selznick. He searched and searched for the perfect actress to play Scarlet O'Hara. The character had leaped off the pages of Margaret Mitchell's book and he could see her in his mind's eye; and he didn't stop searching until he found Vivian Leigh — the perfect Scarlet. Miss Leigh made the character come to life for the movie.

So be sure your character detailing is thorough enough for you to write the next Scarlet O' Hara.

HOW TO WRITE YOUR BOOK   From an Idea to YOUR PUBLISHED STORY   Fleshing Out Your Story

TRIP REVIEW

Map Directions

Character Skeletons Should Be Covered With Flesh

Memorable Characters Deserve Memorable Names

Let Your Words Paint A Picture Of Your Characters

Travel Instructions — Did You?

- ❑ Do Character Detailing for **All** your Characters
      Then add Character Detailing to your
- ❑ Play the Name Game
- ❑ Think of an Actor/Actress who could play the part of your Main Character

OUR WISE GUIDES
POINT YOU IN THE RIGHT DIRECTION

Study characters in books and movies. Don't let your reader say "WHOOO was that character?"

Nobody's perfect like us — Faults make characters more believable and more interesting!

Study your favorite authors. Memorable Characters create page turners and Sales!

◀ **NOTE** ▶

Whether you're interested in publishing or not, Character Detailing will save you time when writing, by helping you keep your characters information straight and accurate. Keep the information in your Travel Folder and use it whenever you refer to your characters

HOW TO WRITE YOUR BOOK   From an Idea to YOUR PUBLISHED STORY   Fleshing Out Your Story

Writing Map 3 — CHARACTER DETAILING — Travel Kit Form

EXAMPLE: Completed Character Detailing

Name: First: Evie Middle: Rose Last: Kane
Age: 18 Date of Birth November 8
Body type or build: Petite, Slim, fine boned
Height: 5'5" **Weight:** 118
Eye color: size/shape: Brown, Pear
Description: Big, Deep Set, very expressive
Hair color/Style: Auburn, Long, Wavy
Skin tone: ☐ Medium
Facial structure: Nose: Small, straight
Lips: Full, even teeth
Face shape: Oval, high cheek bones
General Appearance: Model Like Beauty

Personal Data
Education: Norton University, Majoring - Science
Occupation: Student - Admin. Assist at college
Habits/Traits:
Good: Organized, energetic, caring
Bad: Vulnerable, naive
Hobbies: Designing clothing
Marital Status: Single
Children: None
Friends: Jonathan, Ginger
Likes: Boys, Beach, California
Dislikes: Lying, cheating
Ambition: Model and Design Clothing
Parents: Vivian and Martin Kane
Siblings: Brother, Twin Brad
Background (Ancestors): Grandmother Veronica Lakeland- Model and Spokesperson
Notes: Evie is just studying science to please her parents. Prefers to design her own line of clothing.

Your Main Character:

Name: First:_____ Middle: _____ Last:_____
Age: __ Date of Birth _____
Body type or build: _____
Height: _____ **Weight:** _____
Eye color: size/shape: _____
Description: _____
Hair color/ Style: _____
Skin tone: ☐ Light ☐ Medium ☐ Dark ☐ Other_____
Facial structure: *Nose:* _____
Lips: _____
Face shape: _____
General Appearance: _____

Personal Data
Education: _____
Occupation: _____
Habits/Traits:
Good: _____
Bad: _____
Hobbies: _____
Marital Status: _____
Children: _____
Friends: _____
Likes: _____
Dislikes: _____
Ambition: _____
Parents: _____
Siblings: _____
Background (Ancestors): _____
_____
Notes: _____

HOW TO WRITE YOUR BOOK From an Idea to YOUR PUBLISHED STORY   Locations, Settings & Time

LOCATIONS, SETTINGS AND TIME

The Geographical Location —That's The Place

Once you have established your characters you'll need to put them in a geographical location: country, state, city, town or area where your story takes place. There are two types of locations: the real and the fictitious. When you describe a place that is real it's best to write about a place you know. Some writers prefer to write about exotic places, but if that's your choice, Our Writing Guides strongly suggest: do your research. Today's readers are savvy. They travel all over the world, or have seen pictures, movies, or books about far off places and now can even take an internet trip to check these places out!

The best way to ensure accuracy is to visit the location you want to write about and get a sense of the sights, sounds, smells, and above all—the people. If travel is out of the question, talk to others who've been to your location. Whenever possible communicate with people who live there, get pictures, maps, descriptions and as much information as possible.

31

Imagined Locations

When using a fictitious place, you'll need to draw from a strong imagination. You may have an idea for a locale that is totally imagined or is influenced by a real place. Whenever possible visit that real place. When your location is totally created from your imagination, you can pull out all the stops. The more you can visualize every last detail, the more real that place will be for the reader. If your location is totally imagined, find a quiet place and close your eyes until you can clearly envision all the details of that location. Look around in your mind's eye and then use the Location Detailing, found at the end of this Chapter, as your road map. If that location is fictitious give it a name. Whenever possible, let the name tell something about the place. For example: Peyton Place was named after the founder of the location in a book of the same name. Focus on your main location. Use as many sources as possible to get the clearest picture.

Your words have to bring the place to life!

Remember you don't ever want a reader knowing more about the place in your story than you do!

Get your Writing Map 4 **LOCATION DETAILING** Form from your Travel Kit at the back of this chapter.

Decide on one Main Location - Repeat for additional locations
When Completed store in your Travel Folder

Questions: info@goldenquillpress.com Subject line HTWYB–Map 4

Next complete additional locations: (if you have more than one)

Settings

Once you've established your locations, you'll need to pick a main setting: this could be a house, an office, a park. Start to get familiar with settings by choosing a room in your character's house. Envision that room. Look around: sense the environment, the style, notice the big objects, and then turn an eye to the smallest most interesting accessories. See what this room tells you about the people who live there. If you're using settings that are unfamiliar to you, for example: Sing Sing Prison, visit the prison and the surrounding area. Be sure to talk with the town residents and with prison guards and if at all possible, even the inmates. The more you know about your setting the more realistic it will become. Again if you can't get there, do your research. There are books, movies, and other resources at your local library and book stores. The internet also provides an excellent source of information. If you put in a search for most well known places, you'll get pages and pages of information and sites to visit.

However, if you're using real places such as: "Planet Hollywood," first get written permission to use their name. If you're using a place that doesn't have private ownership, such as The Mississippi River, you do not have to obtain permission.

Permission Now, OR, Lawsuit Later!

HOW TO WRITE YOUR BOOK From an Idea to YOUR PUBLISHED STORY   Locations, Settings & Time

Get your Writing Map 4 **SETTING DETAILING** Form
from your Travel Kit at the back of this chapter.
Decide on one Main Setting - Repeat for additional settings
When Completed store in your Travel Folder

Questions: info@goldenquillpress.com Subject line HTWYB–Map 4

Next do additional Setting: (if you have more than one)

Time

You also need to decide when in time your story will take place. If you're writing about a time period – past or present you may need to research that period to get your details right. The reader won't find your story believable if a character is wearing clothes that didn't exist or driving a car before it was invented. Even when you're writing about a time you are familiar with, and recall events, be sure that all dates and information are accurate.

Realistic Scenes

If your setting takes place in the 1600's, many of the things we take for granted today didn't exist. For example: think of a movie scene, where a woman is wearing a gown with a zipper, but you know zippers didn't exist until decades later. Or, how would it appear if when reading a book set in the early 1900's, the main character is using a cell phone? This error is so obvious you'd know the cell phone doesn't belong. Unless you are writing Sci-fi, stick to realism!

When you're writing about the future you must be sure to create a time period that is different enough, but appropriate for that time. Example: If you were writing about 2030, daily travel back and forth to the moon for work may seem far fetched—but if it were 2210 it becomes much more believable. Create all the elements of that time period, and don't forget to include very vivid descriptions to help the reader grasp that time and can feel like what it would be to live in that time.

Get your Writing Map 4 **TIME PERIOD DETAILING** Form
from your Travel Kit at the back of this chapter.
Decide on one Main Time - Repeat for any additional Time Periods
When Completed store in your Travel Folder

Questions: info@goldenquillpress.com Subject line HTWYB–Map 4

Send your Locations, Settings and Time Periods to the Set and Costume Designer

Before you even begin writing your locations, settings and time periods, you should be sure you've created ones that will be memorable. Think of your favorite movie—and then imagine the story taking place in a different time period – it doesn't necessarily work. Now, think of a scene from your favorite book. Can you close your eyes and picture the way everything comes together — the place, the time and the surroundings.

HOW TO WRITE YOUR BOOK From an Idea to YOUR PUBLISHED STORY   Locations, Settings & Time

If it's a fictitious place see how the name fits, too. That is a well written place and that is what we want you to achieve. Sometimes the most insignificant place leaves a lasting impression, so don't skimp on any details. The best way to check if you've created viable locations, setting and time periods, is to ask yourself some key questions. Could set and costume designers utilize your descriptive paragraphs and know exactly how to create your place, design the sets and obtain the accessories and costumes that are time appropriate.

Put your Main Location, Settings and Time Period in the movies—

 Get your Writing Map 4 Location, Setting &Time Period Detailing Forms. Look over the details and then play Set & Costume Designer.
When Completed store in your Travel Folder
Questions: info@goldenquillpress.com Subject line HTWYB–Map 4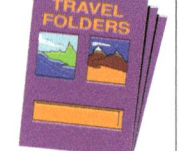

What would the designed set location look like? _____

_____

_____

What would the main designed setting look like? _____

_____

_____

How would your character's be dressed? _____

_____

_____

What accessories need to be present to verify the correct time period? _____

_____

_____

34

HOW TO WRITE YOUR BOOK From an Idea to YOUR PUBLISHED STORY   Locations, Settings & Time

Our Experts Suggest

The Name Game -- Naming Your Imagined Locations

   Once you're sure your Locations are Great, give them Great Names.
If your work is about New York City, then that would be the greatest name you could use,
but if you were fictionalizing New York City, what Great Name would fit that Great City —

How about > > > > > > > >

 Get your Writing Map 4 **LOCATION DETAILING** Form
from your Travel Kit at the back of this chapter.

Decide if the Name of your Main Location is truly GREAT!
- Repeat for additional locations
When Completed store in your Travel Folder

Questions: info@goldenquillpress.com Subject line HTWYB–Map 4

 If you have any questions concerning any topic in Map 4 e-mail tech support
at: info@goldenquillpress.com Subject line: Map 4 Questions

HOW TO WRITE YOUR BOOK From an Idea to YOUR PUBLISHED STORY   Locations, Settings & Time

TRIP REVIEW

Map Directions

Locations, Settings & Time Periods Give More "Flesh" To The Skeleton Of Your Story
Visit Locations Or Do Your Research — Don't Play A Guessing Game
Memorable Locations, Settings & Time Periods Hold the Reader's Interest

Travel Instructions — Did You?

- ❏ Do Location, Setting and Time Period Detailing

    Then add Location, Setting & Time Period Detailing to your

- ❏ Play The Name Game for your Imagined Locations

- ❏ Put your Locations, Settings & Time Period in the Movies

OUR WISE GUIDES
POINT YOU IN THE RIGHT DIRECTION

Study locations in books and movies to help you create exciting places. Don't let your reader say "Who...oh sorry WHERE WAS THAT?"

We are Memorable! Places aren't always Memorable. Create Memorable Locations, Settings and Time Periods by Clawing out the details

Study your favorite authors. Memorable Places make a barking impression!

◀ **NOTE** ▶

Whether you're interested in publishing or not, the Location, Setting and Time Period Detailing forms will save you time when writing and help you keep your information straight and accurate. Keep the forms in your Travel Folders. Use them whenever you need to refer to your Locations, Settings or Time Periods.

HOW TO WRITE YOUR BOOK From an Idea to YOUR PUBLISHED STORY   Locations, Settings & Time

Writing Map 4 — **LOCATION DETAILING** — **Travel Kit Form**

EXAMPLE: Completed Location Detailing

Name: Island Falls

Location: North Eastern United States on the Canadian Border

Type: Town in the New Hampshire

Major Industry: Education (College Town)

Population: 90,000

Average Age Range: 20-50

Average Income: 60,000 Annual

Who Lives There: Kane Family

Address: 220 Maple Street

Background: Old New England town basked in Early American history. Island Falls hosts one of the largest research facilities in the country at Norton University

Describe Location: Island Falls is college town, in the north eastern part of the United States. There are two colleges: Island Falls and Norton University. Surrounded by mountains, this town has a historic downtown core and a rural suburb, inhabited by middle and upper income residents. Compustock is the main shopping mall with brand name stores and quaint shops run by local merchants, including Vid-Mart, a new hi-tech electronics superstore. There is also a large industrial area and a new International Airport.

Your Main Location

Name: _____

Location: _____
_____

Type: _____

Major Industry: _____

Population: _____

Average Age Range: _____

Average Income: _____

Who Lives There: _____

Address: _____

Background: _____
_____
_____
_____

Describe Location:
_____
_____
_____
_____
_____
_____
_____
_____
_____
_____
_____
_____

HOW TO WRITE YOUR BOOK From an Idea to YOUR PUBLISHED STORY   Locations, Settings & Time

 **SETTINGS DETAILING**

EXAMPLE: Completed Setting Detailing

Name: The Cottage

Location: Norton University campus

Type: Secret Facility exterior and interior constructed to look like a Caretaker's House

Who Works There: Martin and Vivian Kane

Setting: A dirt road leads to an unobtrusive structure, called the Cottage, that was specifically designed to resemble a simple caretaker's house rather than the secret science research facility that it houses

Describe Setting: The Cottage, situated on a secure ten acre compound, is totally obscured from view by a thick growth of aged spruce and pine trees, and is not readily visible from the main roads around the campus. Its highly sophisticated fenceless security system prevents visitors and curious students from entering. If someone did wander onto the grounds, the security system would not allow them beyond its perimeter. Added security, cameras, motion sensors and infrared monitors are strategically positioned throughout. The Cottage basement houses the secret research facility operated by Dr. Kane.

Your Main Setting

Name: _____

Location: _____

Type: _____
_____

Who Lives/ Works There:
_____

Setting:
_____
_____
_____
_____
_____
_____
_____

Describe Settings: _____
_____
_____
_____
_____
_____
_____
_____
_____
_____
_____
_____
_____
_____
_____
_____
_____
_____

HOW TO WRITE YOUR BOOK From an Idea to YOUR PUBLISHED STORY   Locations, Settings & Time

 **TIME PERIOD DETAILING**

EXAMPLE: Completed Time Period Detailing

Dates: Sometime in the Near Future

Important Facts:

    Oneness Cards

    V-Tel

    C-Tel

    All Cloning is Outlawed

    International Alliance of Scientists–

    monitors all scientific experiments

    A secret agency monitors all terrorism

    threats - searches for antidotes in

    case those threats become reality.

Describe Time Period: better environmental conditions, longer life spans, eradication of many diseases Scientists work independently, while having the scientific resources of a collective in order to speed up discoveries. But evil, hatred and envy are still forces to be reckoned with. Terrorism is still a major problem for the world, but most countries have vowed to work together to stop all threats. Oneness cards containing all financial and personal information are required for everyone. Technology has made many advances that make everyday life easier. Teleportation systems are being used in big business but might soon be a way to transport people from one place to another.

Your Time Period Detailing

Dates: _____

Important Facts:

Describe Time Period:

Writing Map 5

GETTING ON THE ROAD TO YOUR PLOT

Your skeleton has filled out with the flesh of your characters, locations, settings and time periods. Now, we need to add the life line that holds that body together... the plot. The plot is what begins to bring your story to life.

Plotting is simply the connecting of all the events in your story: the beginning, to a turning point or climax, ending in a resolution. The purpose of plot is to create and control your story idea and all that happens to your characters as the story unfolds. Readers need a reason to care about your story and to want to keep reading. So you need to create situations that will hold their interest.

Our Guides Agree: A Well Devised Plot will accomplish the goals of your story. The plot is the means by which you, the writer: entertain, educate, and satisfy the reader. It's only when there is a clash of forces, and something valuable is at stake, that the reader gets really involved in the story.

Example #1: An escaped convict disguises himself as a priest to make up for his life of crime.

HOW TO WRITE YOUR BOOK From an Idea to YOUR PUBLISHED STORY   The Road To Your Plot

Get your Writing Map 5 **PLOT DETAILING** FORM
from your Travel Kit at the back of this chapter.

Using Example #1 write about your **MAIN PLOT**
When Completed store in your Travel Folder

Questions: info@goldenquillpress.com Subject line HTWYB–Map 5

When structuring your plot, go back to your Map 2 Ideas & Outline Form, review the 5 W's information you've already filled in: now we need to use the What, Why and How.

What: What are the issues: conflicts, complications of your story situations?

Why: Why are these issues important to your story?

How: How are these issues resolved?

Plot pulls all the pieces together!

There are no magic formulas for writing perfect plots. Plotting involves time and development of what works. There are also no infallible rules, but the more you write the easier plotting a story becomes.

Maneuvering Down the Road of Conflicts

You can also create various conflicts to move your story along. Most stories revolve around problems the characters must deal with and solve. These problems will help make your characters more exciting and grip the reader. Problems may arise from inner conflicts, or from situations that occur in your story.

Types of Conflicts
- A character's struggle with the external forces of nature—such as an environmental disaster
- A struggle with some force of society
- A struggle with another individual
- A struggle within one's self
- Goals—advancing in a competitive field
- Overcoming obstacles—such as: poverty, social status
- Health – dealing with physical and mental problems
- Life's turning points – dealing with situations from birth to death
- Motivation and Desire—achievements; winning and losing

Humans Love Conflicts!

Example#2: Bob, a welder for over 40 years was dreading his 60th birthday. That's the day he will be forced to take early retirement.

Get your Writing Map 5 **PLOT DETAILING** FORM
from your Travel Kit at the back of this chapter.

Using Example #2 write about your **MAIN CONFLICT**
When Completed store in your Travel Folder

Questions: info@goldenquillpress.com Subject line HTWYB–Map 5

Twists and Turns

Authors often discover when they begin writing a story that their characters determine the direction the story takes. Good! Listen to your characters. If you understand who they are—their hopes, dreams, goals, conflicts, you will soon find them taking on a life of their own. You may have intended a character to react to a problem in a certain way, then you realize, that character might do it differently. Many authors experiment with plot twists and turns and throw in surprises when they want to help pace the story. But, remember readers are savvy – so, keep your twists and turns believable.

Make sure your Twist doesn't take you on the wrong Turn

Example#3: "How...is this possible? I know you were dead!"

"No, mon ami. I was kidnapped and held prisoner all these years. My capture and reported death were contrived to prevent us from revealing to the world the greatest discovery in recent history."

Get your Writing Map 5 **PLOT DETAILING** Form from your Travel Kit at the back of this chapter.

Using Example #3 write about your **TWISTS & TURNS**
When Completed store in your Travel Folder

Questions: info@goldenquillpress.com Subject line HTWYB–Map 5

Subplots

Subplots are used to support the major story line or theme and to add interest and intrigue. A subplot is a secondary story line or thread related to the main story line. Subplots are interwoven into the action of a story to create connections and complications. Suspense can be created by having several story lines interweaving at the same time. You could consider a love triangle, a test of courage, a power play, or a sacrifice or redemption plot line. You are limited only by your imagination.

Get your Writing Map 5 **PLOT DETAILING** Form from your Travel Kit at the back of this chapter.

Write about your **SUB-PLOT**
When Completed store in your Travel Folder

Questions: info@goldenquillpress.com Subject line HTWYB–Map 5

Flash Forward/Foreshadowing

The **Flash Forward** takes the reader to an event before it happens

Example: Evie finished her design and signed her name. Her upcoming show would be so successful, her parents would finally agree she could pursue a career in fashion, instead of becoming a scientist, like them.

Fore-shadowing is another device that prepares the reader for an event to come, without giving away specific details.

Example: Brian sees Mrs. MixMatcher give Jonathan a coin. He suspects Controller's using the coin to control Jonathan. The BREV Force later discover the secrets of the coin.

Flashbacks

Flashbacks are useful to help fill in details of something that happened in the past. When you tell about past events, if you want to show your characters interacting with action and dialogue, flashbacks need to be written as scenes.

Example: Had it really been 20 years since I met Remy at the Scientist Convention. We talked like two old friends until I learned he was the world's youngest Nobel Prize Winner. That moment changed my life.
Flashbacks/forwards or foreshadowing should only be used when useful to your story.

Get your Writing Map 5 **PLOT DETAILING** Form from your Travel Kit at the back of this chapter. Using the Examples write about your **FLASH FORWARD/FORESHADOWING/FLASH BACK** When Completed store in your Travel Folder
Questions: info@goldenquillpress.com Subject line HTWYB–Map 5

Plot Formulas

Plots have unlimited possibilities, but there are basic formulas that help you get from point A to point B in your story.

Suspense, Success or Dream Goal
Before the main character can achieve his goal, he must overcome obstacles. There's suspense, action, intrigue, and the character may or may not achieve his goal.
    Example: Brad felt Quiz Master attaching something to this head. He knew if he got out, he would never again go up against Controller alone. He finally realized his role in The BREV Force.

Love and Relationships
One of the oldest and most varied plot formulas.
    Example: Jonathan knew he was a nerd and that Evie was out of his league. She was so beautiful, and he loved her so much. He told himself if he could just be around her, maybe she'd fall in love with him.

The Triangle
This is seen in a struggle of two characters for the affection or loyalty of another. This formula, like the love formula, is often used in romance fiction.
    Example: Evie knew she was falling in love with Rick. But she also knew he was rich, gorgeous fast and free...but worse than that he was Sheila's boyfriend.

Redemption:
This involves a change in the character's personality or circumstances.
    Example: Jonathan sat facing Evie. He had lied about the coin, lied about Mrs. MixMatcher. Now he was still lying. Evie was crying and couldn't take anymore. No matter what the consequences, he knew he had to come clean.

Sacrifice:
The sacrifice is seen when the character gives up something dear, even his life for a good cause.

Example: Brad knew he was wrong to go out on his own and try to destroy Controller. He'd made so many mistakes. Now he knew what he had to do. He would take on the most deadly mission.

 Get your Writing Map 5 **PLOT DETAILING** Form from your Travel Kit at the back of this chapter.
Using our Examples write about your **PLOT FORMULAS**
When Completed store in your Travel Folder

Questions: info@goldenquillpress.com Subject line HTWYB–Map 5

Plotting the Course

When you know exactly where your story is headed you will be better able to lead the reader down the roads you choose; roads with conflicts, sub-plots and distractions, and those that lead straight to your destination. Plot Detailing helps you when you begin to write. A simple tool to use to make the plot move is to DELIVER a great story!

USE THE **DELIVER** FORMULA

Devise a problem or issue that exists or is anticipated
Enhance your story by adding complications
Lead to a problem that needs to be solved
Instigate a crisis to overcome
Verbalize dialogue to add realism to a scene
Erupt into a climax
Resolve the problem or issue one way or another

Send your Plot to the Director

Before you even begin writing plot you should be sure you've created one that will be memorable. Think of your favorite movie—and then imagine the whole story taking place around your plot. Now think of a scene from your favorite book. Can you close your eyes and picture how the story would unfold?

A well written plot is what we want you to achieve, so don't skimp on any details. Sometimes the most insignificant plots lead to a great story that leaves a lasting impression.

The best way to check if you've created a viable plot, including sub-plots, conflicts, twists and turns, is to go back to your — Writing Map 5 Plot Detailing Form, and look over the details. Ask yourself whether or not a Director could take your information and know exactly how to make your story into a movie.

HOW TO WRITE YOUR BOOK From an Idea to YOUR PUBLISHED STORY   The Road To Your Plot

Play Director and send your plot to the movies—

What would the advertising slogan be? _____

_____

_____

_____

What would the trailer(promotional piece) include? _____

_____

_____

_____

What one scene would best describe your story? _____

_____

_____

_____

   Have a question about Plot? E-mail tech support at:

info@goldenquillpress.com– Subject line: Plot Questions-Map 5

HOW TO WRITE YOUR BOOK From an Idea to YOUR PUBLISHED STORY   The Road To Your Plot

TRIP REVIEW

Map Directions

Plot Makes Your Skeleton Into A Fashionably Dressed Traveler
Stopping For A Bit Of Conflict Makes For A Better Entertained Reader
Every Road Should Lead To The Resolution

Travel Instructions — Did You?

- ☐ Do your Plot Detailing
  Add Plot Detailing to your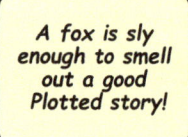

- ☐ Send your Plot to the Director

OUR WISE GUIDES
POINT YOU IN THE RIGHT DIRECTION

"Plot out your plot—Wh— Wh--what was that story about?"

"A fox is sly enough to smell out a good Plotted story!"

"That great Plot even kept the barking dogs quiet!"

◀ NOTE ▶
There's no magic formula for writing perfect plots, but the more you read and the more you practice writing, the better storyteller you will become.

HOW TO WRITE YOUR BOOK From an Idea to YOUR PUBLISHED STORY   The Road To Your Plot

PLOT DETAILING

Writing Map 5

Travel Kit Form

Example Plot Detailing

#1 Main Plot: Computer virus, Controller, headquartered in Island Falls is trying to take over the world. Each member of the Kane Family is working to destroy Controller.

#2 Conflict: Martin and Vivian are working as fast as they can to find an antidote to Controller but time is running out — their children are preparing to face-off with the computer virus and its holograms

#3 Twists and Turns: Brad tries to save Jonathan but he's captured. Evie, Jonathan and Rick try to save Brad and wind up in Controller's mind game.

#4 Sub-Plot: In order to save their friends from Controller Evie and Brad experiment, but it backfires.

#5 Flash Forward/Foreshadow: Martin is stuck in traffic. He wishes he'd phoned Vivian before he left the Cottage. He smiles as he envisions entering their house; she appears at the door as beautiful as the day they met over 20 years before. But a dark cloud intrudes on his thoughts, *How will I tell her about the stranger's visit and her threat to our lives?*

#5a Flash Back: Martin took the notebook from his secret drawer. The sight of the now tattered black book that contained their formula, thrust him back more than 20 years to the day his life changed; the day he met Dr. Remy Marcel.

#6 Plot Formula: A computer virus has turned evil and threatened college student's lives. Martin and Vivian are ordered to find the way to destroy it; while their children prepare to do battle with the entity and its holograms.

Your Plot Detailing

Main Plot: _____
_____
_____
_____

Conflict: _____
_____
_____
_____

Twists and Turns: _____
_____
_____
_____

Sub-Plot: _____
_____
_____

Flash Forward/Foreshadow _____
_____
_____
_____
_____
_____
_____

Flash Back: _____
_____
_____
_____

Plot Formula: _____
_____
_____
_____
_____
_____

Writing Map 6

CONSTRUCTING YOUR STORY

Now that we have all the major elements of your story we're ready to enter our Construction zone.

Structuring Your Story

As with all construction zones we need to take it slow and watch out for caution signs. Getting you safely through this section will take our journey onto a newly paved road. Some writers find, getting those first few words down on paper, the most difficult part of writing. To get you through this complex area, we'll use information we discovered in our workshops. Writers who used our "Detailing Forms," had a better grip on their ideas and easily found their way through the constructing process.

Your Story Beginning

As with all things we must begin at the Beginning. When you read the first few pages of a book, notice how the author begins. Look for ideas that hold your interest and draw you into the story. It could be a setting, a character or a plot, but whatever it is – it Hooks YOU! . And, so it's called, "The Hook."

It's an essential part of writing a book. A hook can be almost anything from a question that must be answered—to a shock scene that leaves the reader wanting more. You can build a place and time that is so fascinating the reader wants to visit often, or you can begin with a love or hate character. Sometimes just mentioning a situation and then leaving it at that, can really make a reader want to hitch hike along with you. Whatever type of hook you choose, your story beginning should incorporate that hook. Be sure you make it strong enough to arouse interest and hold the reader's attention.

Example: Controller, a computer virus has invaded Island Falls and is using this college town's vulnerable young people to achieve it's goals of taking over the world.

Establish Your Hook

My Hook is _____

_____

_____

Onto the Play

Once you've established your "Hook," the next step is to weave it into your story. When you begin to write, it's helpful to visualize how your story will unfold. Just as a play has three acts; stories need to have three segments that divide the action: a beginning, a middle and an end.

The first segment will be the Opening Act: that's where you place your "Hook." This beginning part leads the reader into the story; arouses interest, and holds their attention with the "Hook." This first act should also: introduce the characters, establish the setting, and set the mood and tone of the story.

When the curtain rises on Act II the story should have progressed to the middle. This is where most of the excitement, conflict and intrigue are centered. The tensions should build as the suspense grips the audience and keeps the anticipation high until the curtain falls. This part may take about one half or more of your manuscript to develop. Remember to pace the action; don't put everything in the middle.

The last act is called Resolution. This is the act in which: events and situations are solved, conclusions are reached, loose ends are tied up and any remaining problems are resolved. The outcome or clarification of the plot in a story is called the denouement. Like the final act in a play; when the curtain falls, the audience should be left with a satisfied feeling; the time was enjoyable, understandable and well spent.

Your story can end on a happy or sad note, but it should leave the reader satisfied—not feeling cheated, confused or disappointed. And always remember to tie up all the loose ends. Nothing turns a reader off more than an incomplete ending.

When the ending story leaves the reader with a flash of insight or a sense of understanding, it is called an epiphany ending. Surprise endings are also effective. Just when the reader thinks the story has come to an end—something exciting happens that creates another crisis. We will discuss beginnings and endings in more detail later.

The following diagram that resembles a stage can be a guide to structuring your story.

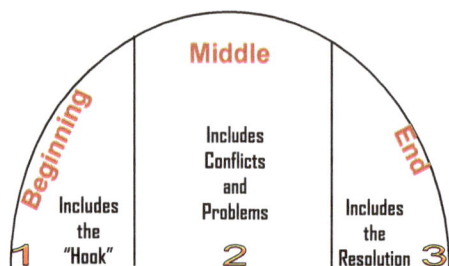

Caught up in Traffic

Converting your ideas into your first draft can be as frustrating as being on a one-lane construction road. You want to get going, but you have to go slow and stay in line. There are many ways to begin this task, but our workshops have provided three techniques that were very helpful to writers: Clustering, Outlining and Story Boarding.
Look over all three and then decide which will work best for you.
First, let's exit at the Drive-In to see how this works.

Let's Go to the Drive-In Movie

If you've ever been to a drive-in movie you know it's basically a big empty parking lot with a huge size movie screen. Well, for our purposes we're going to use that setting to visualize sitting in your car at the drive-in and watching your story unfold on the screen. Visualization is the main key to clustering, outlining or storyboarding. So, get comfortable, relax and get ready to enjoy a great movie — Yours!

First be sure there are no distractions — visualize the drive-in as if you're attending a private screening of your story. Sit back and take some slow deep breaths and clear your mind. Then close your eyes and watch your movie in your mind's eye. The music comes on – the credits appear on the screen and then your story begins.

Allow your thoughts to carry you along as you watch. Trust your instincts — it's your story — without pushing you'll be able to travel from scene to scene. Your story will be shown in chronological order. In many cases, you might want your story to start with a flashback or scene that is disconnected, but for the purposes of our movie, your story will run chronologically.

As you watch the very beginning stop and jot down a few words about what you're seeing. Now return to your visualization and stop at the next major scene. Do the same for every <u>major</u> scene from beginning to end, (you will fill in details later, for now just concentrate on the most important events of your story). Now you should have enough information to begin your story construction. Our Guides want to produce your movie, but they have limited funds. Every scene must be vital to the storyline. Be sure each scene: either develops a character, introduces an element of the story or in some

HOW TO WRITE YOUR BOOK   From an Idea to YOUR PUBLISHED STORY   Constructing Your Story

way moves the story along. If not, throw it out. When you're sure you have all the major scenes, let the drive-in movie run again. Watch the story completely in your mind and let the details begin to fill in. Let the story take on a life of it's own and see where it goes. You may find new characters, settings, and plot twists and turns you didn't think of originally.

Now let's see which method of construction works best for you: (SELECT ONLY ONE)

Choice 1: **Clustering through Traffic**

Clustering means gathering together and we're going to gather your characters, plots and sub-plots, settings etc., so we can visualize how your story will put flesh on the skeleton. We recommend one Clustering Form for each stage: Beginning, Middle and End.

Get your Writing Map 6 **Beginning Cluster Detailing** Form from your Travel Kit at the back of this chapter.

When Completed store in your Travel Folder

Questions: info@goldenquillpress.com Subject line HTWYB–Map 6

Start with your Hook. Put it in the center box. Then decide what events, or elements are most important to the beginning of the story and how they will intersect with the Hook. Write one word in each circle.

Choice 2: **Outlining** your way Around

Another way to gather your story together is to outline. Outlining involves writing a simple sentence for each scene and interconnecting them. Go back to Map 2 your "From Idea to Outline Form." Use your original outline and embellish each scene to cover your beginning and then do the same for the middle and end.

Get your Writing Map 6 **Beginning Outline Detailing** Form from your Travel Kit at the back of this chapter.

When Completed store in your Travel Folder

Questions: info@goldenquillpress.com Subject line HTWYB–Map 6

Choice 3: Stopping at the Beach for some **Storyboarding**

Storyboarding is a technique used in the movies and television to lay out the scenes to be filmed. It's a series of pictures and/or notes arranged to chart the flow of the story. In writing we use a similar storyboard to lay out the major sequences from beginning to end. A storyboard will give you a visual picture of how your story unfolds and connects Chapter to Chapter. If you already have your story written you can use storyboarding to check continuity and review scenes: for pacing, plot twist, character development and sometimes even to change how the scene unravels. To use story-boarding you will need either index cards, (white and colors), a chalkboard and white and colored chalk, or large oak tag (also called poster board) and colored pencils. You'll also need to set up an area that allows you to view your scenes in a continuous manner — for index cards, pin or tape them to an empty wall, corkboard or on a large oak tag/poster board.

NOTE: Our Writing Guides Suggest:

THE INDEX CARD SYSTEM IS THE SIMPLEST METHOD. FOR OUR PURPOSES OUR EXAMPLE WILL USE THAT SYSTEM.

Start with approximately 20 white index cards. Each card will represent a major scene. Either draw or jot down enough information to visually depict that scene.

Next, take your colored index cards and write the filler that leads each scene to the next. Your colored index card # 1A would fill in the interim events between Card #1 and Card #2. You can also expand your storyboarding to include vital information. One color for other main character's, one color for sub-plots. Soon, you'll see a pattern. The white cards may represent chapters and the colored ones are for the details that take you from one chapter to the next.

EXAMPLE: Index card #1 A woman mysteriously arrives at Martin's office and orders him to work for the government.

> Index card #2 Martin hides papers in his home office which contain the illegal experiments he's secretly been working on.
>
> Index card # 1A On his drive home Martin pictures his pregnant wife and decides not to tell her the details of the papers in his briefcase.

Our Writing Guides Suggest:

We know you're eager to begin writing, but there's still a great deal of information that will assist you in writing your first draft — that will save you time in editing and revising – so be patient and you'll be rewarded.

HOW TO WRITE YOUR BOOK   From an Idea to YOUR PUBLISHED STORY   Constructing Your Story

SAMPLE Storyboarding Diagram to assist you with what your final storyboarding should look like.

Code: White - major scenes — Yellow- character info
          Gold- Subplots — Blue- important info to interject

Free Writing

Once you've maneuvered through the miles of construction, your next traffic slow up will be Free Writing. The purpose of Free Writing is to take your Clustering, Outline, or Story Board and convert it to the written word. Free writing is connecting the dots with words. Short burst of words or thoughts connect the Hook to your story's beginning. Free writing is whatever comes into your mind; you don't get stopped by punctuation, dialogue or in depth description, and the only rule in this session is stick to the Clustering, Outline or Story Board. This is your way to cross the bridge from ideas to actual writing, without having to worry about the formalities. This bridge doesn't have a toll and it takes your vehicle from a one-lane constructed road to a three lane written highway.

Get your Writing Map 6 *Free Writing Detailing* Form and your *Beginning Cluster/Outline or Story Board Detailing* Form from your Travel Kit at the back of this chapter.

When Completed store in your Travel Folder

Questions: info@goldenquillpress.com Subject line HTWYB–Map 6

53

Don't forget to use each point. You may also find that as you begin to write you may add other factors that had never occurred to you before.

Are you feeling a Draft

Now, we are ready to take your Free Writing and turn it into your first draft. Here are some tips to help you prepare. Use these keys to start your writing engine:

"C's" Keys 1 mile

The words often called keys to good writing begin with "C."

CLEAR	**CONCISE**	**CONSISTENT**
CORRECT	**COMPLETE**	**CONSCIENTIOUS**
	CONTINUITY	

CLEAR -
The English language has been developing for centuries and new words are added every day. Unless you're writing a period piece, try to use words your readers will understand. Always say exactly what you mean. Let's examine clichés; those old expressions can sometimes clutter a writer's work. Here are a few:

> **Example:**
> Last but not least   Smart as a whip   Clear as a crystal
> Music to my ears   Cool as a cucumber   Pretty as a picture
> Raining cats and dogs Easy as pie   Sharp as a tack

There are hundreds of clichés. Don't let them dull your writing. Choose words that are fresh and expressive.

CONCISE -
Conciseness in writing means to write without using long words (several syllables) when a simple word will do.
> **Example:** Incorrect – "I'm going to my residence, then I'm going to retire."
> **This sentence is wordy and pretentious. It'd be better to say:**
> <u>Correct</u> – "I'm going home, then I'm going to bed."

CONSISTENT -
Means to stay within the same tense
> **Example:** Incorrect – "We went to visit a friend, but she is not there."
> **This sentence shifts from past tense (was) to present tense (is).**
> <u>Correct</u> – "We went to visit a friend, but she was not (wasn't) there."

> **Number and Person.**
> **Example**: Incorrect – "We went to a play one knew would be dull."
> **This sentence shifts from first person plural (we) to third person singular (one).**
> <u>Correct</u>: - "We went to a play we knew would be dull."

COMPLETE -
When telling a story, it's important to include facts the reader would not know. Remember the reader is not in your head so spell it out! Use specific words for clarity.
> **Example:** Incorrect –"She was angry, she picked up something and threw it."
> **The sentence did not indicate who was angry; what item she picked up or why she threw it.**
> <u>Correct</u> – "Mary was angry with Tom because he was late for dinner. She picked up an apple and threw it at him."

CONSCIENTIOUS -
Words help to portray different characters through description and dialogue. Language that's appropriate for one character may be all wrong for another. For instance, the reader expects the vocabulary of an educated professor to differ from that of a hip teenager.
> **Example:** (Professor) – "I'll examine all the possibilities and get back to you at a later date.
> (Teenager) – "Dude, I'll check it out and ketch ya later."

Conscientious writing also examines character gender. Try not using "He" when a job is done by men and women. Writers often solve this problem by using gender free writing: Barbara is the new mailperson.
> To avoid gender-specific language, try these suggestions:

Instead of:	**Use Gender-free Writing:**
Mankind	People
Salesman	Salesperson or Representative
Businessman	Executive or businessperson
Foreman	Supervisor
Fireman	Firefighter
Workman	Worker

CORRECT –
Finally, read through your work line by line searching for errors in punctuation, spelling, structure and over all clarity. Use pronouns and nouns instead of starting a sentence with "IT" or "THAT."

CONTINUITY—
One of the most important aspects of any story is continuity. Keeping your facts straight and always making sure you know where everyone and everything should be at all times.
> **Example:** Martin searches frantically for his lost keys and finally finds them on the small table in the hallway. He shakes his head, *How could I have missed seeing them <u>they were the only object on the table</u>*.

(Next scene) Rushing out the door, Martin looks around for his keys and finally spots them; <u>glittering next to a heavy glass candy dish.</u>
If the keys were the only object on the table, then how could they be glittering next to the candy dish?

CONTINUITY CONT'D —

Example: Brad put on his <u>blue suit</u> in preparation for his court appearance.

(Next scene) When Brad is introduced to the District Attorney, he shakes hands then removes his <u>grey jacket</u>.

How can Brad be wearing a blue suit with a jacket that's grey?

Facts are so important to keep straight — so don't let the reader catch you being Incontinent. Oh inconsistent?

Example: Martin went downstairs and signaled the code that unlocked the secret laboratory. <u>He entered and closed the interior door</u>.

Next scene) Martin heard the "intruder alert" and <u>ran out of the lab and up the stairs</u> to the building entrance.

Martin never opened the interior door to go upstairs

Well, by now we're sure you are experts on the "C's," so now it's time to park your car for the night and take a well deserved rest— get some "Z's."

The next step of your trip will be writing your first draft!

HOW TO WRITE YOUR BOOK   From an Idea to YOUR PUBLISHED STORY   Constructing Your Story

TRIP REVIEW

Map Directions

Clustering, Outlining & Story Boarding Keep Track of How Your Story Will Evolve

Free Writing Speeds You Through The Construction Zone

Drafts: The Vehicle That Road Tests Your Story

Travel Instructions — Did You?

- ❒ Do Clustering/Outline/Story Boarding
- ❒ Do Free Writing
- ❒ Add the forms to your
- ❒ Remember the "C's" Keys

OUR WISE GUIDES
POINT YOU IN THE RIGHT DIRECTION

Your Great Hook might even Catch an OWL!

Learning About Your Craft y Is The Smart Fox Way to Get Started!

First Draft— Second - Third - keep barking up that tree 'til you get it right!

◀ **NOTE** ▶

Following all the road maps and taking your time through the Detailing, Clustering/Outlining/Story Boarding and Free Writing will save time when you begin writing your Drafts.

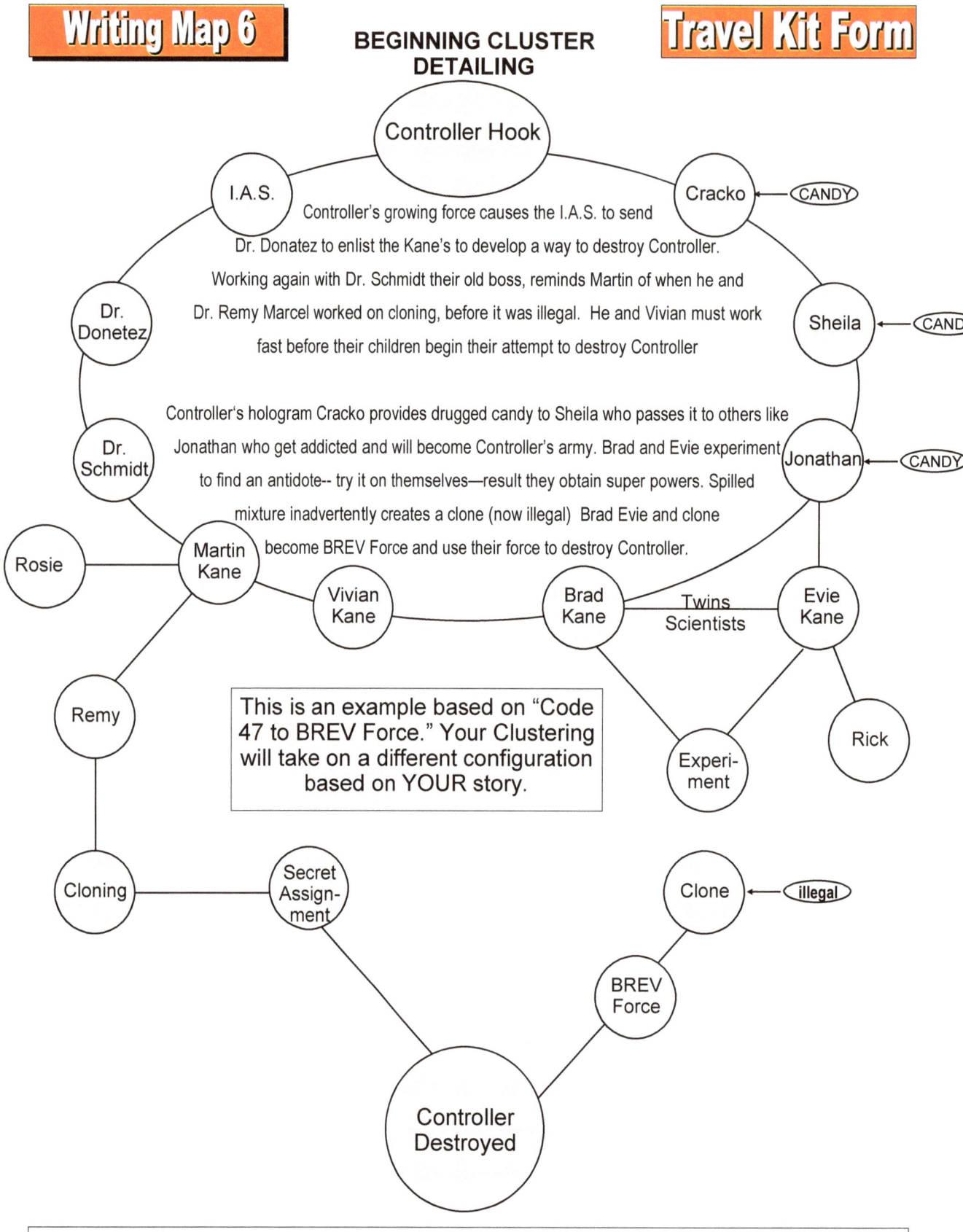

HOW TO WRITE YOUR BOOK   From an Idea to YOUR PUBLISHED STORY   Constructing Your Story

Writing Map 6

BEGINNING OUTLINE DETAILING

EXAMPLE: Original OUTLINE
A computer virus has grown beyond its original programming and has invaded the small college town of Island Falls. Controller has programmed holograms to do its bidding and to persuade college students to join its ranks.
Scientists Martin and Vivian Kane are recruited to stop Controller. Their children's (Brad and Evie) best friend, Jonathan, becomes hooked by Controller's forces (hologram Cracko and human helper Sheila) and Brad and Evie strike out on their own to defeat Controller.

EXAMPLE: Story Beginning OUTLINE
Controller, a computer virus has grown beyond its original programming and become more than a virus –
Headquartered in Island Falls, a 2 college town, gives Controller a lot of possible recruits for its evil.
Controller uses holograms, first one – Cracko—like a drug dealer—and Sheila, human convert to deal out mind altering drugged candies.

The I.A.S. an international scientific agency has been monitoring this computer phenomenon.
They send Dr. Donatez to persuade the Kane's (Martin and Vivian) to develop a way to destroy Controller
They will be happy to be working again with their old boss, Dr. Schmidt. It has been years and that thought reminds Martin of when he met Dr. Remy Marcel and worked on cloning—it was legal then

Brad and Evie Kane's friend Jonathan is one of Controller's recruits.
Fearing for Jon's life, they use their scientific knowledge to try and find an antidote to the drugged candy, but when they try it on themselves it gives them abilities. During the experiment, some of the formula spilled and inadvertently created a clone. Knowing the legal ramifications the clone is concealed and with Brad Evie become BREV Force and vow to destroy Controller.

Martin and Vivian must work fast to find the way to destroy Controller, before their children face off with it.

Your Original OUTLINE:
_____
_____
_____
_____
_____
_____
_____

Your Story Beginning OUTLINE:
_____
_____
_____
_____
_____
_____
_____
_____
_____
_____
_____
_____
_____
_____
_____
_____
_____
_____
_____
_____
_____
_____
_____
_____

Writing Map 6 — FREE WRITING DETAILING — Travel Kit Form

Example Free Writing Detailing

Martin opened his e-mail

< "R U the 1" >

"somehow I've been *targeted for this garbage, but how?*"

e-mail account maintained through a high level security server SPAM factors set at highest priority security level password protected code was necessary for incoming mail also an auto blocker for any non verified e-mails. world's most secure server? Order ROSIE *find out how it gets through and where its coming from* New Homeland Security warning from General Babcock website, www.natsecurity.classified.gov set up list suspected terrorist

    Kane's ordered to work with Dr. Schmidt to destroy Controller by Dr. Helena Hidalgo Donatez of ISA

    Martin calls General Babcock and then the President

    Controller invades Island Falls campuses hologram Cracko turns students into loyal army

    Jonathan becomes follower— Brad and Evie experiment — clone created and super powers— go up against Controller and Cracko

Your Free Writing Detailing

_____

HOW TO WRITE YOUR BOOK   From an Idea to YOUR PUBLISHED STORY   The Rear View Mirror

LOOKING THROUGH THE REAR VIEW MIRROR

Before we begin our journey today we need to decide who is going to drive. As the narrator, or one who tells or writes the story, you must decide from whose point of view your story will be told. That will be your designated driver.

Choosing your View--point

A story told in the first person uses the pronoun "I" throughout the story. This viewpoint allows the reader to get into the writer's head or to see through the eyes of the major character. Memoirs and personal experiences, tend to work best when written in the first person.

First Person Viewpoint: The writer tells the story:
  Example: "I remember the first time I met Remy."
     The writer tells the entire story
     from this **"I" viewpoint.**

The first person viewpoint has its advantages because it allows you to deal with one mind — as if following the events of a story with a camera; relating what you see.

HOW TO WRITE YOUR BOOK   From an Idea to YOUR PUBLISHED STORY   The Rear View Mirror

`A word of caution: the disadvantage of first person viewpoint is that you can't get into the minds of other characters — you're writing what you see, hear, feel, and experience.

First Person Character's Viewpoint: <u>One Character tells the story</u>.
    Example: My name is Dr. Helena Hidalgo and the town I come from is Hidalgo Mexico, named for my ancestors.
The main character can't tell you anything from another character's point of view

Second Person Viewpoint: <u>The Who Speaking is "YOU"</u>
   Second person viewpoint is where you address the reader directly. It's a difficult, but not impossible concept; generally not recommended for first time novelists.
    Example: When **you're** sound asleep in the middle of the night, and the telephone rings, **you** wonder who could be calling.
Second Person Viewpoint <u>Used in non-fiction, "How-to" articles, and recipes</u>
    Example: **You** need 4 ripe tomatoes, 2 small onions and 1 teaspoon of salt. **You** blend all ingredients...and so on.

Third Person Viewpoint:

<u>Through the eyes of many characters.</u>

Third Person Viewpoint is told through the eyes of one character at a time. The narrator knows the thoughts, experiences and feelings of that character and all the other characters and when speaking uses the **characters name** or "**he**" or "**she**." No matter how many characters tell their viewpoint, the entire story should be told in third person.

Best View for beginning writers

    Example: Martin walked back into his main office. He was bewildered by the odd events of Dr. Donatez's mysterious arrival, "Rosie, pull up her 'Oneness' information, I want to check her security clearance."

Point Your reader to the Right View

(another character's point of view)
"I'm way ahead of you," she replied, "so I did some additional checking. But, other than her 'Oneness,' all information is classified top secret, 'Eyes Only'." She thought for a moment — *maybe I'll just hack my way in!*
(When the character speaks the character says "I")

As the story unfolds, we follow the characters through the eyes of the narrator. We see what they say, do and think and how they relate to others in the story. Third person viewpoint is often favored by beginning writers because it's easy to control.

Choosing a viewpoint depends on the kind of story you're writing. If you want to tell the story as if you are experiencing the events, choose first person. When you want to interact with all the characters, use third person viewpoint.

There are also more advanced and complex viewpoints, such as:

Third Person Limited Viewpoint: <u>Limited to One Character</u>
   Example: Evie ran as fast as she could toward the main campus where her car was parked. She got in and locked the door. She was shaking. *Why was Brad acting that way?* A knock on her window scared her half to death. "Brad!" she screamed, opening the window and holding her heart, "You could've killed me!"

   "What's wrong with you? I saved you!" he said.

The third person limited viewpoint is widely used by authors, especially in short stories. This viewpoint limits the narrator to the feelings, experiences and thoughts of only one character. That character can, however, draw out the thoughts, feelings and ideas other characters express through the use of dialogue.

Third Person Omniscient Viewpoint allows the author to tell the story as if he's watching it unfold. This is often called the <u>"God" viewpoint.</u> <u>The narrator sees all, knows all, and can take the reader anywhere; in any or all of the character's minds.</u>

In the following, the narrator tells what each character does, thinks, feels and says.

   Example: Evie knew Brad was a great researcher and if anyone could figure out what was in that strange candy, he could.
   Once inside the lab Brad found the materials he needed to analyze the ingredients of the candy.
   Sheila waited outside the lab praying they wouldn't learn the truth.

Now that you know enough ways to point your view

Get your Writing Map 7 **VIEWPOINT DETAILING** Form
from your Travel Kit at the back of this chapter
decide which point of view works for your story
When Completed store in your Travel Folder
Questions: info@goldenquillpress.com Subject line HTWYB–Map 7

First Draft

You're finally through the construction zone and have your view pointed in the right direction; so now you're ready to get on the super highway of writing. This is the road that turns your Free Writing into your first draft. The draft is the preliminary rough road to your story. Authors often write and rewrite several drafts before they're satisfied with the finished work.

 Go back to Your Travel Folder Writing Map #6 and get your *Free Writing Detailing* Form. Read it over and then:

Fill up your tank with your ideas and use them to get back on the road again. Only this time instead of Free Writing: use structured sentences, embellish with description, add dialogue and let's get up to speed. Once you get through the first few Chapters of your first draft you have green lights to continue through that draft to the end of your story.

Your goal is to write your story so it will flow from beginning to end in an entertaining, organized manner. Following this road will lead to some tips for writing sentences, dialogue, description and more in the next few Writing Maps:

So, Let's Start Beginning the Beginning:

HOW TO WRITE YOUR BOOK   From an Idea to YOUR PUBLISHED STORY   The Rear View Mirror

TRIP REVIEW

Map Directions

First Person Viewpoint Is Often Favored For Non-Fiction "How-to" Books & Articles

Third Person Limited Viewpoint Is Often The Story Tellers Choice

Omniscient Viewpoint Can Be Useful As A Way To Control Your Characters

Travel Instructions — Did You?

☐   Choose Your Viewpoint

☐   Add to your

OUR WISE GUIDES
POINT YOU IN THE RIGHT DIRECTION

◀ NOTE ▶

Choosing the right viewpoint helps you show and tell your story more effectively.

Writing Map 7 — VIEWPOINT DETAILING — Travel Kit Form

First Person Viewpoint Detailing

The writer tells the story:

"I remember the first time I met Remy. I never would have imagined he was the youngest noble prize winner.

Character's viewpoint.

My name is Brian Vincent Kane, the name my family gave me when I went to live with them.

Second Person Viewpoint Detailing
Direct to the Reader

When **you're** lying awake in the middle of the night, **you** can hear every sound; every tick of the clock, and rain drop against the window pane.

Third Person Viewpoint Detailing
Character's point of view

Brad's mother, Vivian wanted to cry. She felt all her son's hurts.

(When the character speaks the character says "I")

"I wish you would talk to your father, Brad. Maybe he would understand why you did it. You know I do."

Limited
One Character's View

Evie knew something was wrong. Her emotions were getting in the way and she couldn't reach Brad's mind. **She** decided to try again. "Code 47, Brad please respond?"

Omniscient
Any and all character's views

Brian was sure Controller was still alive and time was running out to prove it.

Brad couldn't help but wonder why Brian was still so obsessed with Controller.

Evie wished she knew what was going on with Brad and Brian.

Choose Your Person Viewpoint Detailing:

_____

MECHANIC--ISM'S OF WRITING

Our editor guide Ms. Edi Tor will be taking you through the mechanics of writing. Even though we call your first formal writing a "draft," you still need to understand the mechanics. A first draft is your rough plan, put down on paper with the intention of being revised into the final manuscript.

Our Writing Guides Have Issued this Draft Alert!

Some writers can write a book the first time, but most writers need several drafts; editing and revisions. So let's assume that the first writing is a draft! When you are traveling on your writing journey and feel a "draft," you would stop and let a trained mechanic examine the problem. So here's what the Mechanics of Writing recommend to diagnose your Draft.

Choose Your Writing Venue

Writing Long Hand:	**Writing on a Typewriter**	**Writing on a Computer** (This example uses MS WORD)
• Lined paper 8.5 X 11	• Blank, Paper White 8.5 X 11	• Open Word & start with a blank document
• Write on every other line	• **Margins** – 1 inch around	• Go to **"File"** (top far left) left click NEW – then click on **Page Set-up** – (this opens a window) under **Margins** you will see top, bottom, left and right. You can set your margins at 1" around and be sure your **Page Orientation** is set to **Portrait**
• Write on only one side of the page	• **Indent 5 spaces**: beginning lines, quotes & new paragraphs	
• **Indent 5 Spaces**: beginning lines, quotes and new paragraphs	• **Double Space**	**SAVE** –Name the file **"Draft"** Save in either in **My Documents** or on your **Desktop.**
• **Number** your pages	• Type on **only one side** of the page	• Start each new **chapter** on **separate page-** 1/3 down the page -Chapter # or Chapter Title
• Start each new **chapter** on a **separate page**	• **Number** pages	• Under Format (in the top header) left click, then click on **Font** – Choose: Arial or Times Roman, Font Style: Regular, font Size: 12 and color Automatic or Black.
• **Make copies** whenever possible (copies can be made at libraries or post offices or office supply retail places that have copy machines)	• Start each new **chapter** on a **separate page** for 1/3 of the way down	• Under Format (in the top header) left click, then click on **Paragraph**—Under Line Spacing click on Double
Make up a Draft Folder and always put your work in there (Note: Final Manuscripts must be in typewritten or computerized format)	• **Make copies** (Use carbon or NCR paper, or go to the library or post office, or office supply retail places that have copy machines) Make a Draft Folder and always put your work in there	• **Indent 5 Spaces**: beginning lines, quotes, and new paragraphs
		• When you finish your writing sessions **Save** your work and back-up your work
		• Blank white 8.5 X 11 paper (for draft printing)
		• Print on only one side of the page
		• Print only on White Paper – Black Ink
		Make a Draft Folder and always put your work in there

Now that Our Mechanic has given you the spec's for set up— to begin writing your first Draft, use the Mechanics Technical Manual found below which includes directions for different techniques to help you begin your story.

Techniques from the Mechanic

Writers use many different devices when beginning a story. If you want your reader to go further than the first ten pages this is your "15 Minutes of Fame." The beginning of your story can make or break you. So let's make it so exciting the reader can't put it down. There are many openers that work, but of course you need to find the one that works for your story. Here are our Mechanics Choices:

CHARACTER

Open with the main character doing something that gets to the meat of the story: saving the world, going into pre-mature labor, committing murder, even falling off a cliff
    Example: Brad knew he was wrong, but all he could think of was, *if I can fix this, I can destroy Controller and save Jonathan's life.*

If your character is going to save the world you could begin with the action
    Example: *Brad had to make the most of his jail time. He broke into Controller's network files while the guards weren't looking. He knew if he got caught it would be the end of everything...*

Or try fast paced dialog specific to the action
    Example: "Evie what's going on?"
               "Oh, Rick. I believed this was a real job, but now they have pictures of me that they are threatening to put on the internet…"
               "I won't let them hurt you. Sheila knows a lot of people and…"
               "Sheila!" she screamed. "I should've known better that to trust you! Just go away and leave me alone." she ran out the door.
               What the...! Evie, Sheila, women, they're all crazy. Or maybe it's me?

Bring your character into the scene
    Example: Island Falls was beautiful at this time of year, but Dr. Schmidt wasn't interested in the beautiful scenery Vivian and Martin pointed out. All he wanted was to get into the lab, get what he came for and leave.

SCENES
Scene openers can be enticing to a reader. Be sure you establish the reason for the scene.
    Example: Vid-Mart was the latest electronics super store to open at Compustock Mall. Brad enjoyed working there because all the great looking girls from both colleges in the town eventually came in for something.

DESCRIPTION

Describing the day, a character, or event is another way to begin. Don't get too long winded on description if it doesn't move the story along.

> **Example:** The leaves were kicking up in the wind, on that chilly autumn day. It reminded Martin that he would soon be raking up the dirt that his lies would leave.

TIME PERIODS

You can begin your story in the past, present or future. You can also start with a chapter about something that happened long ago or will happen in the future, that seemingly has nothing to do with your story. You can lay the groundwork for the event that will be pivotal in your story, an event which you don't mention again until you are ready to tie things together later. That later chapter is called the Pivotal moment.

> **Example:** Opening Chapter- 1912 The Titanic sails from England and sinks
> Next Chapter - 2008 Martin and Vivian two interns meet at the Science Institute
>
> Pivotal event - Later Chapter - Martin and Vivian marry and are planning their honeymoon. He suggests a cruise. She nearly faints at the thought. Through her tears she tells him her grandfather was killed on the Titanic.
> He can't believe it, his Grandmother was too!

DIALOGUE

A phrase that will be repeated or will have significance throughout the story
> **Example:** "<R U the 1?>"

Or, introducing a conversation, mid-stream
> **Example:** "I understand that emotions limit our abilities, but I can't help it."

No matter how you begin your story it's essential that you hook the reader and that you set the tone and style of the story, right from the beginning. Examine the writings of modern authors such as: Jeffrey Archer, Patricia Cornwell, Tom Clancy, Clive Cussler, John Grisham, Tami Hoag, Stephen King, Johanna Lindsey, James Patterson, Sidney Sheldon, Danielle Steele or return to the classics of: Jane Austen, Charlotte Bronte, Charles Dickens, Mark Twain or Leo Tolstoy, but whoever you choose, look for the hook and the tone and style they set.

CHAPTERS

Years ago if you would've asked how long a chapter should be, the answer may have been - - the longer the better. Today that's no longer the case. Recently we have even seen a long time best seller: "The Da Vinci Code," by Dan Brown, where a chapter was a page long, or less. Using good judgment is probably the best answer. If you're moving your story from: one central character to another, to a new location or a different time period, these changes should be reflected by a new chapter. You can also use chapters to create cliff hanger endings or to take your story in another direction.

MECHANICS MANUAL OF PUCTUATIONI

When you speak face to face with another person you have more than words alone to make your meaning clear to the listener. Your facial expressions, gestures, body movements, tone of voice, and pauses all influence the meanings of words you speak. But when you write you don't have all of that going for you, so what do you do?

The primary aim of writing is to communicate with the reader, and this is why punctuation — a kind of roadmap — was established. The rules of punctuation have been standardized by educators, writers and editors for more than a hundred years, to make writing as clear and coherent as the spoken word. When you use correct punctuation, the reader can understand words and their meanings. For example, when speaking, you pause and hesitate, and when writing, you use the comma to pause, and the period as a full stop.

Too much punctuation can be as confusing as too little. You should use just enough to make your story flow easily and as naturally as if you were speaking. Reading your sentences aloud will help you see where you may need to correct punctuation.

The Mechanics Manual of Punctuation
Note: For easy reference; punctuation will be put in

BOLD RED

Period (.) is used at the end of a complete sentence. It is also used as the end mark for initials and many abbreviations.
> Mrs. Smith sent her manuscript to a publisher in Trenton, N.J.
> The editor was impressed by J. T.'s short story.

Comma (,) is used inside sentences, in places where one would pause while speaking. It is also used to set off many phrases and clauses, and should be used before end quotation marks.
> Tom found his car in the parking lot, only to realize he had lost his keys.
> "I have a new bike," John said.

Question Mark (?) is used at the end of an inquiry, or a sentence that asks something.
> "Do you know who won the baseball game?"
> "How did the editor like your manuscript?"

Exclamation Point (!) Is used to convey stronger-than-usual emotion or urgency. It can also follow certain interjections instead of a comma.
> "How dare you say that!"
> " Hey! That's my car!"

Quotation Marks (" ") are used to express a direct quote, to   enclose slang and technical terms. Use an open quote mark(") at the beginning of the quote and a closed quote mark (") at the end. Quotation marks are also used to enclose titles of poems, stories, essays, articles, chapters of books, songs, and radio and television programs.

Jeff said to me, "I knew you were up to something."
My favorite song is, "America The Beautiful."

Punctuation that refers to the quote stays *inside* the quotation mark. Remember that quotation marks are used to enclose the actual words of the character and the punctuation.

Inside: John said, "Who saw the kitten last?"

Computer users please note: When you begin a quote, (since there is only one quote mark on the keyboard), do the following: **Shift"** to type the first quote mark, then type, (no space) and at the end of the quote: **Shift"** (no space after last letter). You can see the beginning and end quote marks fall in the proper directions. (If you don't use this procedure or if you leave a space between the quote and the first or last letter, the marks will be in the wrong direction).

Single Quotation Marks (' ') are used to enclose a quote within a quote.
"I heard John say, 'Be sure you get home by six'."

Apostrophe (') expresses the possessive forms of most nouns/pronouns.
    Singular: a girl's gloves —
    Plural ends in s, the ' follows the s: the girls' gloves.
If the plural noun doesn't end in *s*, such as men, add an apostrophe and *s*:men's.
    The apostrophe is also used in contractions, to show that letters have been omitted and for personal possession. Here are 2 examples:
    He couldn't believe how big the mountain was. (contraction of could not)
    Tom's book is fascinating. (possession)

Colon (:) is used before a list, to identify the speaker in plays and scripts, and before a formal statement.
    (list) My mom told me to pick up three items: soap, shampoo, and toothpaste.
    (identify the speaker) Juliet: Romeo, where fore art thou Romeo?
    (formal statement) The agreement states: We agree to the terms.

Semicolon (;) is used to separate parts of a list and as a more pronounced break in long sentences. It can also be used between incomplete sentences that are not joined by a conjunction (and, but, or, etc.) or by a conjunction adverb (however, indeed, etc.). Think of the semicolon as more than a comma and less than a period.
    My birthday is June 29; Mary's is September 7.
    We thought the band was entertaining; others thought the show was boring.
    Our costs were: tires, $25; fuel $50; oil $20.25.

Hyphen (-) is used to designate a continuation of a word that has been divided at the end of a line. When used to continue a word, one-syllable words should not be divided, and multi-syllabic words should be divided between syllables.

>Evie regretted not knowing the modeling job was like walking into Controller's evil web. If she had thought about it she wouldn't have gone.
>My lunch break is usually around a half-hour.

Dash (--) is used to indicate an abrupt change of thought or flow in the sentence. It is also used to introduce a phrase that summarizes the rest of the statement. (use only 2)

>The three P's --)planning, preparing and persisting -- are the keys to success.
>Respect, good teamwork, a love of the game -- these are the qualities that make champions.

Parentheses [( )] enclose extra information, or description, that's not relevant enough to the sentence to require a comma. Sentences that contain parentheses should read as well without them as they do with them.

>John's cat (the brown one) likes catnip.
>I added salt (sea salt) to the recipe.

Ellipsis (...) omission of a word or words necessary for a complete construction of the sentences but understood. The dots (...) form a punctuation mark indicating the omission of a word or words or change of thought, but understood by the reader. Three periods indicates the omitted words, but then continues. Four periods indicates the omission comes at the end of a sentence.

3 periods ...   There is something more to do ... but that can wait.
4 periods ....   This is all we have to say....

Punctuation and Writing Dialogue

Punctuation can be tricky when you write dialogue. Dialogue should reflect the spoken words as closely as possible. When writing dialogue, indent five spaces (as a paragraph) for each line spoken by a character.

>See example of spaces (_____) = 's 5 spaces
>>Two friends meet at a restaurant to discuss a problem one of the women is having.
>>_____ "John works late every night," Myra said as she sipped her coffee.
>>_____ "Have you told him how disappointed you are when he doesn't come home for dinner?"

You can see how indenting makes dialogue easier to read. Also, notice how this conversation flows without repeating "she said" tags after each character speaks? Tags are often necessary to show which character is speaking, but don't overwork them. Instead use description.

Colons and Semi-colons Within Dialogue

Generally, colons or semicolons are not used within dialogue.
> Greg wanted to go to Stonebrook College; his father insisted he try West Point first.

But in dialogue you'd write:
> Greg said, "I want to go to Stonebrook College!"
> His father insisted, "Greg you will go to West Point first."

The Dash and The Ellipses In Dialogue

You can use the dash to punctuate a line of dialogue interrupted by an action
> "You played very well, Sally" -- she waved her hand -- "I'll see you later."

You can use the ellipsis to show speech that trails off.
> "If you don't come out of the pool this instant, I'll . . . ."

Numbers In Dialogue

Spell out numbers in dialogue.
> "He'll be here at two-thirty," Joyce announced.

For dates and other long numbers it is acceptable to use numerals.
> "The license number on the new car is 13882," the police officer said.

Writing Numbers

When writing numbers, it's easy to make mistakes. As a general rule, numbers 10 and under are spelled out;
> My three brothers are on the baseball team,

Spell out numbers one through ten, except when there is a series of related numbers.
> The girls sold 2 boxes of cookies, 3 dozen candy bars, and 16 bags of popcorn.

Use numerals for numbers over 10
> More than 300 people attended the conference.

Always write out numbers at the beginning of a sentence.
> Three hundred and twenty-five shirts were packed.

Or don't start a sentence with a number
> We packed 325 shirts.

Always spell out numbers at the beginning of sentences even when other numbers are present.
> Fifteen children, 10 boys and 5 girls, were in the class.

Numbers in the thousands, millions and above are generally spelled out.

> Old Paul claims that over the years he has saved over two million dollars.

Statistical numbers can be digits
> By March 3, 1999, more than 17 stores closed. A survey revealed that only 10 had moved to other locations and 7 had filed bankruptcy.

Less statistical writing

> Three years ago, Marge decided to sell seventy acres of her thousand-acre farm. She closed the deal in January, 2001.

HOW TO WRITE YOUR BOOK From an Idea to YOUR PUBLISHED STORY Mechanic-isms of Writing

If you want to Practice Writing Numbers STOP on the side of the road and Review the routes. Decide whether the correct answer is the numeral or the word.

She owns at least _____ cats.
Would the answer be:　　　　　5 or five?

There were _____ players.
Would the answer be:　　　　　35 or thirty-five?

The   boy's   were   age   _____, _____ and _____
Would the answer be:　　　　　3 or three , 8 or eight　　　11 or eleven

Paul owes _____
Would the answer be:　　　　　$2,000,000.00 or two million dollars

SEE Answers Upside Down

Corrected Sentences and Explanations

1. She owns at least *five* cats. (Numbers 10 and under are generally spelled out)
2. There were 35 players. (Numbers above 10 are generally written as numerals)
3. The boy's ages are 3, 8, and 10. (Numbers under 10 are written as numerals when there is a series of related numbers)
4. Paul owes over *two million* dollars. (Numbers in the thousands, millions and above are generally spelled out)

Frequently Misspelled Words

Sound out the word!

It's easy to misspell words because so many words sound alike, but nothing makes a work look amateurish as much as misspelled words. Misspelled words should be rare, if at all. Use a Dictionary. Now you ask if I don't know how to spell, how do I look up the word to spell. Suppose you're unsure about the word vacuum. When you say the word you think... Sometimes Spell Check in a Word program will help you or try searching the internet for the meaning rather than the spelling!

Or just ask Cortana or Siri

V A Q U M

Begin to look up as many letters as possible in the dictionary that have these letters — Start with Va   next try and look for the "q" sound. If q is not the next letter try a similar sounding letter — c or k. And, so on, until you find the word vacuum. (see below)
Then read the definition to be sure you have gotten the right word.

→
> **va·cu·i·ty** (vækjú:iti:) *pl.* **va·cu·i·ties** *n.* the state or quality of being vacuous ‖ something pointless [fr. L. *vacuitas*]
> **vac·u·o·late** (vǽkju:ouleit) *adj.* vacuolated **vác·u·o·lat·ed** *adj.* containing vacuoles
> **vac·u·ole** (vǽkju:oul) *n.* (*biol.*) a minute cavity in cell protoplasm containing air, sap or partly digested food ‖ a small cavity in organic tissue [F.]
> **vac·u·ous** (vǽkju:əs) *adj.* having or showing a lack of understanding or intelligence or serious purpose ‖ emptied of content (e.g. of air or gas) [fr. L. *vacuus*, empty]
> **vac·u·um** (vǽkju:əm, vǽkju:m) 1. *pl.* **vacuums**, **vac·u·a** (vǽkju:ə) *n.* a part of space in which no matter exists ‖ a space largely exhausted of air ‖ space containing air or gas at a pressure below that of the atmosphere ‖ (*pl.* **vacuums**) a void, *her departure left a vacuum* ‖ (*pl.* **vacuums**) a vacuum cleaner 2. *v.t.* to clean with a vacuum cleaner [L. neut. of *vacuus*, empty]
> —Aristotle insisted that a vacuum was an impossibility, using this argument to explain the cohesion of a solid, and this dogma persisted for

We all have Sirten— GROWL -Certain words we tend to misspell ugh— MISSPELL

When working on a computer be aware of issues with Spell Check. (Note: When a word can be spelled differently depending on the definition, you need to be extra careful to use the correct spelling. Such as to, too and two, or there and their. The computer might show the word as spelled correctly, but **Our Guides Suggest** you also run a Grammar Check which might highlight the Error. The best answer is to read your work carefully. We also suggest using a professional editor to be sure your work is presented professionally to a publisher.

The Misspelled Words list is a Construction Zone Slow Down Flag to keep you aware of Commonly Misspelled Words as you're writing. Add the words you tend to misspell and refer to the form often when writing.

Get Your Writing Map 8 **MISSPELLED WORDS** Form

And review the most popular misspelled words.
When Completed store in your Travel Folder

Questions: info@goldenquillpress.com Subject line HTWYB–Map 8

Punctuation /Spelling Test Drive —

Get your Writing Map 8
PUNCTUATION /SPELLING TEST DRIVE *Form

Correct the punctuation in the paragraphs
When Completed store in your Travel Folder

Questions: info@goldenquillpress.com Subject line HTWYB–Map 8

DON'T PEAK

When you finish *Map 8 Punctuation/Spelling Test

Find the Corrected Version

On the page after the form

So Don't Go AHEAD and Peak!

Your Reference Library

When professional writers need to look up the spelling or meaning of a word or other information, they don't guess — they look it up! All writers need a good reference library, but just having the materials is not enough. You need to use them! Refer to your Dictionary often. Many good dictionaries also have additional information such as: abbreviations, thesaurus and reference information.

When you want a different word; a more defined word, look to your Thesaurus. This reference contains thousands of synonyms and antonyms, plus sample sentences to help you find just the right word.

Books with historical information are becoming more and more of a necessity to writers. It's important to use correct terminology and language and to accurately describe all aspects of any time period you write about. Reference material such as one of the books we've published, "Tell It To The Future," is a compilation of stories and timelines that depict life in each decade of the Twentieth Century. visit http://www.goldenquillpress.com/bookstore.html

Travel Guides are worthwhile when choosing an unfamiliar location.

A writing handbook is a valuable addition to your library for letter writing styles, writing numbers or other business related information.

Build your reference library with good reading materials. The more you read and study, the better you'll write.

HOW TO WRITE YOUR BOOK From an Idea to YOUR PUBLISHED STORY Mechanic-isms of Writing

TRIP REVIEW

Map Directions

Whatever Vehicle You Use, Don't Forget The Mechanics Of Writing

Use The Mechanics Technical Manual As A Reference When Writing

Punctuation Helps Your Characters Speak For You

Travel Instructions — Did You?

- ❐   Review your Technical Manual
- ❐   Add your Misspelled Words and Punctuation/Spelling Test Drive to your
- ❐   Update your Reference Library

OUR WISE GUIDES
POINT YOU IN THE RIGHT DIRECTION

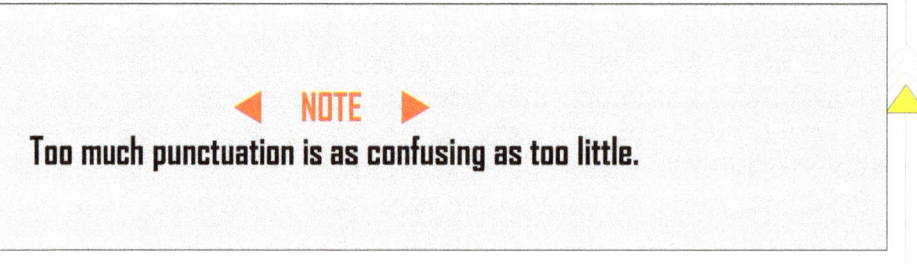

◀ NOTE ▶
Too much punctuation is as confusing as too little.

HOW TO WRITE YOUR BOOK From an Idea to YOUR PUBLISHED STORY Mechanic-isms of Writing

Writing Map 8 — CORRECT SPELLING FOR COMMONLY MISSPLELLED WORDS — Travel Kit Form

acknowledgment	forge	professor
advertisement	friend	quandary
agreement	gauge	receipt
analysis	grateful	receive
anniversary	hoping	reference
apologize	hypocrisy	renown
arctic	independent	respectfully
asinine	ingenious	restaurateur
background	innate	sentence
balloon	inoculate	separate
bastion	judgment	sincerely
battalion	liaison	sophomore
bookkeeper	liquefy	subtly
business	lose	superintendent
ceiling	marshmallow	supersede
cemetery	minuscule	threshold
complexion	moccasin	tragedy
controversy	owing	truly
correspondent	pastime	until
disagreeable	pharaoh	
dissipate	poinsettia	
fluorescent	proceed	

ADD YOUR FREQUENTLY MISSPELLED WORDS

_____   _____   _____

_____   _____   _____

_____   _____   _____

_____   _____   _____

_____   _____   _____

_____   _____   _____

_____   _____   _____

_____   _____   _____

_____   _____   _____

Writing Map 8 — PUNCTUATION / SPELLING TEST DRIVE — Travel Kit Form

Now that you understand punctuation and spelling, take this paragraph for a Test Drive.

Correct all punctuation and misspelled words.

His reaction each time he saw this e mail was the same   Crazy How does this keep getting through   Martin s e mail account was maintained through a high leval security server   Totally frustrated he opened the intercom sistem to the Cottage   Rosie it got through again   How s it possible He didn t wait for a response   Well I no longer want to deal with this and want an answer by the time I get there

Her reply was immediate And good morning to you too boss What a great way to start my morning we should try this more often I m sure it would increase the day s production by at least 100%   However if I knew how the e mail magically got through this server s maximum security wall I would ve told you

But since we keep getting this e mail asoome   whatever   Then know I can t stop it   I m doing my best I am the BEST and will continue to tirelessly work on finding the solution Until then I sirtainly don't need to start my day this way and if I may say so Dr K neether do you

   Well yes uh   I ll be in shortly

SEE CORRECTED VERSION Next Page

This is the Corrected Version

Map 8 Punctuation/Spelling Test Drive

His reaction each time he saw this e-mail was the same. Crazy! How does this keep getting through? Martin's e-mail account was maintained through a high level security server. Totally frustrated he opened the intercom system to the Cottage. "Rosie, it got through again! How's it possible?" He didn't wait for a response. "Well, I no longer want to deal with this and want an answer by the time I get there!"

Her reply was immediate, "And good morning to you too boss! What a great way to start my morning. We should try this more often, I'm sure it would increase the day's production by at least one hundred percent. However, if I knew how the e-mail magically got through this server's maximum security wall, I would've told you.

"But, since we keep getting this e-mail; assume...whatever. Then know: I can't stop it, -- I'm doing my best, (I am the BEST), and will continue to tirelessly work on finding the solution. Until then, I certainly don't need to start my day this way, and if I may say so Dr. K. neither do you...."

"Well, yes uh... I'll be in shortly!"

Writing Map 9
CHARACTER'S SPEAK UP

As a writer your words bring your story to life. Giving your characters the right voice is important; it's how they speak. You give your characters voice by use of vocabulary; choosing the right words, and then creating tone by how you handle dialogue. A character who is 80 years old, obviously, would not speak in the same voice as a child, or a young person.

Take the following situation and see if you can pick out who's saying what

Four people: a three year old boy, an elderly woman, a businessman, and a young mother, all have the same experience. Each stumbled on a piece of broken concrete on a sidewalk. Their dialogue should identify which of these people is speaking:

1. "Ouch! I fall down and hurt my toe." _____

2. "Why can't this city repair these sidewalks? We pay enough taxes!" _____

3. "Oh, my, I didn't even see that hole in the sidewalk. I could've fallen and broken my hip!" _____

4. "Someone's child is going to fall down and get hurt." _____

SEE ANSWERS—NEXT PAGE

Answers: (1-five year old boy; 2-business man; 3-elderly woman; 4-young mother)

Identity Clues - Would the mother say" "Ouch! I fall down?

Read the sentences again to see how the choice of words and punctuation helps you set the tone in dialogue.

Creating Realistic Dialogue

You may read a story with little or no dialogue, yet the narrator has made it so interesting and compelling that you know how your characters are relating and communicating. However, in most stories, authors have their characters speak. They balance description and dialogue to move the story along.

You may be able to paint fascinating word pictures, such as describing the many colors of a rainbow at sunset, but be aware of overworking description. Today's readers like action and dialogue — a fast read!

Dialogue can be used to create tension, heighten suspense and to intensify conflicts. Dialogue can reveal a character's inner emotions, goals and motivations. Dialogue is also used effectively as a devise for pacing a story.

Tension and Conflict

Example: Mary was not in the mood to sit at home night after night.

"I'm not going out, I'm tired after a days work." Tom said.

"Well! I'm not cooking dinner. I sit home all day and I need to get out of this house. I'm going whether you come with me or not!" Mary grabbed her coat and handbag.

"You can open a can of beans," she shouted as she slammed the door behind her.

There's so much tension I can't speak - gur--edit

This scene shows tension and conflict in conversation. If you wrote this scene without dialogue, would you be able to visualize the tension and conflict expressed by the characters, Mary and Tom?

Dialogue and Setting

Example: The Kane's were relocating to Island Falls and looking for a new home.

"There it is, Mom!" Evie said. "That white Colonial with the pillars and black shutters. Dad, pull into the driveway." Evie was bubbling with excitement.

"Look, it has a three car garage," Martin laughed, "Room enough for my workshop."

"And the landscaping must have cost a fortune—and look the backyard has a flower garden, too." Vivian had dreamed of having more than a few potted plants on a window sill. "I can't wait to see it."

Does the dialogue help you visualize the house? Could you portray the emotions felt by The Kane's without the dialogue?

When you feel your story is becoming bogged down, you can use dialogue to speed up action. If the story is moving at a faster pace than it should, you can slow it down by having you character engage in conversation or thoughts that seem natural.

> Rebecca had waited until her husband finished his coffee before she spoke. "Cal, I'm so sorry, but ...I'm leaving you."
> Cal paused to collect his thoughts before speaking. After a long silence, he looked up at Rebecca, "Why has it taken you so long to speak up?"
> Rebecca avoided looking at her husband of 30 years as she tried to think of how she could explain why she was leaving him.

You can see how this dialogue has slowed the pace by using words such as: paused, long silence, avoided and waited. Faster pace words might include: hurry, excited, interrupted. When using dialogue to control pacing, choose words that reflect what your characters are experiencing.

 Get your Writing Map 9 **DIALOGUE DETAILING** Form
from your Travel Kit at the back of this chapter
When Completed store in your Travel Folder
Questions: info@goldenquillpress.com Subject line HTWYB–Map 9

List 5 words that Slow the Pace and 5 Words that Speed Up the Pace

_____ _____ _____ _____
             _____
_____ _____ _____ _____
             _____

Use the Active Voice

The way you write a sentence and your choice of words can make your writing dull or give it color and dynamic impact. When you write in the passive voice, you tend to become wordy and your writing loses its quality and effectiveness. The active voice is less wordy and has a more positive tone.

        Passive: The car was driven home by Helen.
        Active: Helen drove the car home.

        Passive and wordy: It was agreed that John should be recommended
                                      to our publisher and this has been done.
        Active and concise: We all agreed to recommend John to our publisher.

        Change the following to the active voice:
            Passive: A house is being built by John Smith.

Active: _____

Passive: In the yard the children are playing.

Active: _____

SEE ANSWERS UPSIDE DOWN

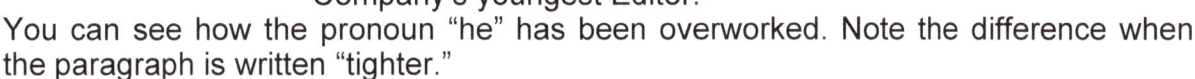

Answers: 1. John Smith is building a house. – 2. Children are playing in the yard.

Nouns and Pronouns – Person, Place or Thing

When writing about a specific person, avoid over-working pronouns "he" or "she."

    Example: John began **his** new job after **he** moved to California. **He** enjoyed working with **his** colleagues and **he** soon became leader of **his** team. **He** soon moved up in the company, where **he** became Ace Company's youngest Editor.

HE, SHE, IT No, Edi Tor, Fox!

You can see how the pronoun "he" has been overworked. Note the difference when the paragraph is written "tighter."

    Example: John began a new job after moving to California. **He** enjoyed working with **his** new colleagues and soon became the team leader. John is Ace Company's youngest Editor.

On the other hand, it can become boring to the reader when you eliminate all pronouns and always use the noun.

    Example: Sara was going shopping. **Sara** drove to town where **Sara** met her friend, Liz, and **Sara** lunch. After **Sara** called her mother to tell her she would be late.

Here's a better version:

> **Sara** was going shopping. **She** drove to town where **she** met her friend, Liz, and they went to lunch. After lunch, **Sara** called her mother to tell her she would be late getting home.

The careful use of nouns and pronouns helps the reader visualize and identify characters as your story progresses.

Verbs: Action Words--Past, Present and Future

The verb expresses action; a condition or state of being. When writing a story, it's easy to get caught up in telling the story and forget to watch verb tenses. The reader needs to have an understanding of when an action is taking place. When writing, be sure to check verb tenses as you progress.

Principal Parts of Verbs

Present	Past	Past Participle	Future
Break	Broke	Broken	Break
Choose	Chose	Chosen	Choose
Do	Did	Done	Do
Drive	Drove	Driven	Drive
Know	Knew	Known	Know
Speak	Spoke	Spoken	Speak

 Write the present, past, past participle and future of the word "write"

_____   _____   _____   _____

SEE ANSWERS UPSIDE DOWN

Answers: Write, wrote, written, write

You can't always say do, did, done, do... sometimes you need A FUTURE Perfect Tense—like, will be!

Tense	Use	Example
Present	to show what is happening now	I **write** stories.
Past	to show what happened at a time in the past	I **wrote** poetry when I was young.
Future	to show what will happen in the future	I may try to **write** a novel some day.
Present Perfect	happened in the past and continues in the present	I **have written** from my garden for years and I like **writing** there.
Past Perfect	happened in the past even before another action or event	The book **was written** before the editor approved it.
Future Perfect	something that has not yet happened, but will before some time in the future	By Monday the instructor **will have written** all the lessons for the week.
Present Continuous	an event that is happening now	I **am writing** new stories everyday.
Past Continuous	to show an event happening when something else happens	I **was writing** when my computer crashed
Future Continuous	something will happen when something else takes place	The author **will have written** the ending before finishing the manuscript.

Additional Review of Verb Tenses

Adjectives and Adverbs

Overworking adjectives and adverbs can clutter your writing with pretentious wordiness.

Adjectives - Describe or identify nouns and pronouns, (person, place or thing).
    This cake is delicious
    The adjective *delicious* describes the noun *cake*.

Adverbs - Describe verbs, (action words) and other adverbs. Adverbs answer the question of when, where, how, to what degree or extent.
    When: We saw her an hour ago.
    Where: We marched onward.
    How: He spoke glowingly
    Extent: She could hardly hear me.

Words can often be over-worked— Exceedingly – Really – Very -- Hopefully – That
Here are A Few and Our Suggestions:
    Overworked —The weather was exceedingly pleasant.
      BETTER   The weather was pleasant.
    Overworked — He really likes baseball.
      BETTER   He likes baseball.
    Overworked — The cake is really very good.
      BETTER   The cake is delicious.
    Overworked — We will hopefully get there in time.
      BETTER   We hope to get there in time.
    Overworked — People think that dogs are fun pets.
      BETTER   People think dogs are fun pets.

Dialogue Tags – License Plates for Dialogue

Tags have one purpose in dialogue — to identify the speaker. Common examples of tags are "he said," or "she said." When tags are used after every line of dialogue, they detract from the imagery you're trying to create for the reader.

"I'm going to work, see you tonight" he said.

"When you come home we can discuss dinner," she said, hoping he would suggest going out for their anniversary.

This conversation is dull and boring. You don't need to use "said" in every line.

Description can create a better and more natural flow.

"I'm going to work," Bob called out as he picked up his car keys and headed for the garage.

"Do you want to have dinner at home or shall I meet you somewhere?" Jan responded, trying not to show how disappointed she was. Bob had forgotten their anniversary.

"I'm in the garage, and can't hear you." Bob snickered to himself. Looking at her anniversary present; a new car. He opened the door and suggested, "Jan, can you come out here. I want to show you something."

We've used descriptive action to replace he said, she said. Telling what the character is doing, makes your dialogue more interesting and moves your story along better at the same time. When writing dialogue, weigh each word carefully for meaning and remember an occasional "he said" "she said" works too.

Writing Dialogue

At times, tags, such as, "He said" or "She said" may be all you need to make your characters and scenes come alive.

When you feel you need more colorful and descriptive words, refer to Your Travel Folder Map 9 TAG LIST Form for ideas and add words you can use instead of said.

   Get your Writing Map 9 **TAG LIST** Form
from your Travel Kit at the back of this chapter

When Completed store in your Travel Folder

Questions: info@goldenquillpress.com Subject line HTWYB–Map 9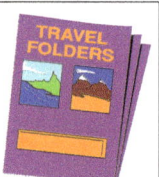

Create a story without "he said, she said." Experiment with words that will adjust the pacing; slower and faster. NOTE: When 2 people are speaking you do not need to identify the speaker, unless the dialogue is getting very long. When several people are speaking you must identify who is speaking to keep it clear for the reader.

 Add your suggestions for replacing "he said" "she said"
E-mail: info@goldenquillpress.com subject other "Said" words

Using the Best Meaning

Use words to express what you mean as you paint word-pictures for your reader. A sentence can fall flat or it can create strong imagery, purely by your choice of words. Stronger words leap off the page:

Strong Action Words: Choose which expression you would use:
Mary is annoyed and expresses her emotion by:
Closing the door behind her.
Slamming the door behind her.
Shutting the door behind her.

_____

Correct Answer:
Mary would **slam** the door because if she is annoyed she's more likely to express her emotion with the stronger action.

Using Formal and Informal Words

Just as you dress appropriately for different occasions, you need to choose the right words for the kind of piece you're writing. At times the more formal word works — other times the simple word works better.

formal -- He will ascertain if the document is legal.
simple -- He will find out if the document is legal.

Formal	**Informal**
deceased	dead, passed away
endeavor	try
facilitate	make easy
in lieu of	instead
residence	home
sufficient	enough
terminate	end, stop
transpire	happen

Rhythm and Flow

Reading your work aloud and tapping (like a drummer), you can hear the rhythm and flow. You can also tape yourself and check the playback. There's no set rule for sentence length, but be cautious when your sentences seem too long or too short. When sentence after sentence is short and choppy, your writing becomes monotonous.
Example: Johnny ran home from school. He wanted to see his grandma. She was coming to visit. She always brought lots of presents.

Running sentences on and on without punctuation can be just as annoying as short choppy ones.

Example: Johnny ran all the way home from school because he couldn't wait to see his grandmother who was coming to visit and Johnny knew she would be bringing lots of presents and he was happy.

Whew! When a sentence runs 20 to 30 words or more, dissect it to see where you can use punctuation.

Example: Johnny ran all the way home from school. He couldn't wait to see his grandmother who was coming to visit. He was happy because he knew she'd be bringing him presents.

Tightening the Seat Belts

Cut out excess words, paragraphs, even chapters that are not relevant. Follow these detours and tighten up.

Fix these overly wordy sentences

1. Wordy: When you have finished your work, you can then go home.

_____

2. Wordy: That was the very same cat that I saw jumping on the chair.

_____

SEE BETTER ANSWERS UPSIDE DOWN

Answers: 1. Better: When you're finished, go home. 2. Better: That's the same cat I saw on the chair.

The Right Word Turning Signal

The English Language contains many words that are similar in either sound, or meaning. When you aren't sure which word is right - look it up.

Get your Writing Map 9 **RIGHT WORDS** Form
from your Travel Kit at the back of this chapter

When Completed store in your Travel Folder

Questions: info@goldenquillpress.com Subject line HTWYB–Map 9

Use this list often when writing to be sure you
Write the Right Word for Your Right Meaning!

HOW TO WRITE YOUR BOOK   From an Idea to YOUR PUBLISHED STORY   Character's Speak Up

TRIP REVIEW

Map Directions

Dialogue: Controls Pacing, Creates Tension, Heightens Suspense & Intensifies Conflict

Dialogue Gives the Reader Personal Involvement In Your Story

Description Is important, But Dialogue Moves The Story Along

Travel Instructions — Did You?

- ☐ Scout for License Plate Tags to use instead of "He Said," "She Said"
- ☐ Watch your Detours and places to pay attention to "The Right Words"
- ☐ Add Writing Map 9 Forms to your

OUR WISE GUIDES
POINT YOU IN THE RIGHT DIRECTION

Formal or Informal Let Who's Speaking Decide

Read Dialogue Aloud to be Cunningly sure Your Characters Sound True to Life

Active Voices Barking Makes for well Paced Dialogue and —A Great Read!

◄ **NOTE** ►
Dialogue is the means by which your characters communicate.

HOW TO WRITE YOUR BOOK   From an Idea to YOUR PUBLISHED STORY   Character's Speak Up

Writing Map 9 — DIALOGUE DETAILING — Travel Kit Form

EXAMPLE: Dialogue Detailing

Just then, Jonathan and Rick came busting through the door. "We came to make the odds more even," Jonathan boasted.

"You are late for this exam." Quiz Master shouted at the two boys. "If you do not find your seats in one minute, your will both be marked absent and will: A. Fail,   B. Fail or,   C. Cause Brad here to have a very nasty accident.

Jonathan and Rick quickly found crates and sat down.

Quiz Master then informed them, "Now, you boys did not do your homework, or you would have known that when you opened the door, you tripped an electronic devise," the hologram laughed. "The common term, for your edification, might be: A. bomb, B. false alarm, C. electrical explosive or   D. booby trap or not …. This is of course multiple choice, but which ever you choose, A, B, C or D the timer is counting down the destruction of this warehouse as we speak.   Oh such fun," the hologram danced around, "this is turning out to be an incredible lesson. Everything and everyone will be destroyed. That is, of course, except me!"

Phoenix wanted to get everyone out of the warehouse to safety, but without knowing what other disasters might be triggered, he did not dare.   He signaled Dove who was keeping an eye on a very distraught Sheila. "What about me?" Sheila moved away from Brad and positioned herself between Quiz Master and the class.

"Sorry my dear, the casualties of being in this class, you know! You are expendable along with your other classmates. Sometimes it is necessary to make a point so everyone can learn, and if you must go too… ah well!"

Dialogue Detailing:

_____

HOW TO WRITE YOUR BOOK   From an Idea to YOUR PUBLISHED STORY   Character's Speak Up

Writing Map 9 **TAG WORDS** **Travel Kit Form**

A
added
agreed
answered
asked

B
barked
bellowed
blurted
boasted
bubbled

C
commanded
commented
complained
continued

D
declared
defended
demanded
directed
drawled

E
emphasized
exclaimed
explained
exploded

G
gasped
giggled
grinned
groaned
grumbled

H
hissed
hollered
howled
hummed

I
insisted
interrupted
invited

J
joked

L
laughed

M
moaned
muttered

O
ordered

P
persisted
pleaded
protested

Q
quipped

R
recalled
related
replied
responded
roared

S
said
scoffed
scolded
shouted
sighed
snapped
snickered
snorted
spoke
sputtered
stammered
stated
suggested

T
teased
thought

U
urged

W
whimpered
whined
whispered
wondered

Y
yelped

ADD YOUR OWN TAG WORDS

_____   _____   _____

_____   _____   _____

_____   _____   _____

_____   _____   _____

Writing Map 9 — USING THE RIGHT WORD — Travel Kit Form

Affect/Effect
Affect means to influence.
Her unhappiness affected us.
Effect means to accomplish;
The effect will be known soon.

Amount/Number
Amount - bulk quantities
They dumped a large amount of soil on the street.
Number - countable quantities
There were a number of birds on the lawn.

Bad/Badly
Bad - not good
This is a bad apple.
Badly - poorly done or felt
The work was badly done.

Can/May
Can - ability to do something
I can go to school today.
May - permission to do something
You may go to the movies.

Cheap/Inexpensive
Cheap - implies shoddiness
Cheap fabric won't wear well.
Inexpensive - less costly
Inexpensive fabrics will last.

Distrust/Mistrust
Distrust - lack of faith, suspicion
I have reason to distrust him.
Mistrust – lack of confidence
I mistrust what the ad claims.

Feasible/Possible
Feasible - practical
That is a feasible plan.
Possible - able to be done
It is possible to solve this.

Few/Less
Few - things counted
I have fewer days to work.
Less - things measured in other ways
We used less water today.

Foreword/Forward
Foreword - comment at the beginning of a book
I will write the foreword to the book.
Forward - movement toward a point in time or space
Move the chair forward.

Further/Farther
Further - refers to time
Further along in the project we'll have more time.
Farther - refers to distance
The house is farther down the street.

Irregardless
DO NOT USE THIS WORD
Instead Use regardless:
We will progress regardless of obstacles in our way.

Its/It's
Its - possessive form of it
The bee stored its honey.
It's - contraction of it is
It's time to go.

Lay/Lie
Lay - to put something in place
Lay the books on the table.
Lie - to repose
You should lie down.

Like/Such as
Like - similar
This doll is like yours.
Such As - used when referring to specific persons, places, or things
Houses such as these are rare.

May/Might
These two words are interchangeable, but might connotes slightly more uncertainty than may
You might want to eat lunch early.
You may want to eat lunch early.

Me/I
NOTE: Very Easy To Confuse so do the test: Where are You?
HINT: Reverse the answer such as:
Me am here   or   I am here
Or make it singular
Go with John and me. Go with John and I.
HINT: Take off John and see.
Go with me.   or   Go with I.
Of course me is correct.

Site/Cite
Site - location
They will build on this site.
Cite - to call attention to
We will cite him for bravery.

This/That
This - something close by
This is my coat.
That - something more remote in distance or time
I intend to buy that coat next week.

Who/Whom
(Whom is the objective form of who).
Jan, whom I spoke with earlier today, called back.
I don't know who lives next door.

Your/You're
Your means belonging to you.
It is your book.
You're – contraction of you are
You're the best friend I have.

Writing Map 10

YOUR WRITING STYLE

You're not born with a writing style, it's something you develop as you begin to write. Your style is your manner of expressing your ideas and thoughts; distinct from other writers.

Writers have been known to try to imitate the writing styles of famous writers such as Jane Austin, Pearl Buck, Charles Dickens, Ernest Hemingway or others whose books continue to sell year after year; or modern writers, such as: Clancy, Grisham, King, Meyer, Patterson and Rowling. What imitators fail to realize is that a painting by Picasso differs from a Van Gogh. The same is true for writing styles. Your writing style uses language that expresses your visions so your reader hears, sees, feels, and senses not only the magic of your words, but all the meanings they convey.

Take Your Style via the Highway of Emotion in Tone

When you speak, your voice has a tone that expresses emotion and enhances the meaning of your words. You use a different tone of voice to express anger than to express joy. When writing, your choice of words and how you punctuate sentences helps convey the mood you want to set. Tone is the overall mood you establish in your writing to make your story come alive on the page, and it's a valuable tool when writing dialogue.

Read the following sentences aloud to see how punctuation and word choice can change the tone and mood of the same sentence.

"I'm going to work," she said.
"I'm going to work!" she shouted.
"I'm just going to work." she explained.

Practice writing for tone. You've lost a favorite item or a large sum of money. Express your disappointment in two sentences. Give the first sentence a little emotion and the second express everything you're feeling. Read your sentences aloud, and see if you have written the emotions into the tone.

_____

_____

_____

Turn onto the Highway of Tone via Description

Tone in writing is not limited to dialogue. You can set the tone (and mood) by the words you use to describe just about anything. If you wrote, "It was a dark and stormy night," this opening line sets a tone by describing the weather.

In contrast, you might write, "It was a bright, sunny day in spring. Birds were singing and flowers were blooming." These sentences set the opposite tone.

You can see that consistency is important. If you were to write: "It was dark and stormy and the birds were singing," it would be confusing. But, if you said the sunny day turned into a dark and stormy night, that would be a good lead in for a change in tone.

It's important to keep the tone of your writing consistent and to be careful when you change the tone.

> The baby was laughing as his mother sang to him, then all of a sudden, he began to cry. She held him on her shoulder, patting his tiny back. "Go to sleep," she cooed, but the baby cried louder. Suddenly, she felt the tiny body stiffen. Her baby was choking—turning blue. Holding the struggling child with one arm, she raced to the telephone and dialed 911.

Mixing tone comes out all chewed up--

This short scene shows how tone can change within a scene. Here, the scene begins with a happy tone, then changes to one of fear and anxiety. If you were to write this story from beginning to end, the under-tone would be the mother's love and concern for her child.

 Finish this story and change the tone back to joy as the baby's life is saved. Use your description and dialogue to show anxiety and fear turning to relief and happiness.

_____

_____

Transitioning from one road to the next—Use the Bridge!

Transitions are the bridges you use to get from one thought to the next. They are the connecting roads that lead the reader from one paragraph to another and one chapter to another. Transitions are necessary to keep advancing your story in a natural flow. Without transitions your main theme can get lost, especially in a long article or novel. In movies, transitions occur as a scene ends and is then picked up again, at another time or place. When writing a story, transitions help you manage dates and time; move your characters from place to place and help you avoid having to write out every small detail.

The Time Transition Technique

This short example uses time transitions to move the story along. Visualize Annie and what has happened in her life, past, present, and what she sees for the future.

Every day began at dawn for Annie. She had to care for the farm animals, cook; do all the household chores, and keep the books for the thousand-acre farm where she lived with her father. (This paragraph introduces the character in the present time. The following paragraph is the transition to the past)

Annie's mother had died five years ago, in a tragic accident. Her mother had gone to take her father his lunch. As she ran beside the tractor to hand the lunchbox up to him, the machine swerved, striking Annie's mother. Annie's father blamed himself for the death of his wife and over the years he had changed into a bitter, fault-finding old man. (Now the transition will bring the character back to the present and shows the effect of the past.)

Annie tried to talk about her mother with her father, but he refused any conversation, so Annie did her chores during the week and planned outings to get her out of the house on Saturdays. This Saturday she would do her shopping, then meet Danny Roberts at the ice cream store. Her heart was breaking. Danny's father had gotten a new job and his family would be moving to California. Someone else she loved would be leaving her life. (The following paragraph sets up another transition. Now we are stating the present time.)

Saturday morning, Annie happily started down the stairs, but her father was waiting with the car keys in hand. "I'm driving into town today," he growled. "There's not gonna be a trip to the ice cream store for you Missy Anne, so don't think you're gonna see that Robert's boy. Not today and thankfully, not ever again."

During the two-mile trip into town, Annie fought back the tears. She had to get to Danny!

 Practice writing transitions, continue the story by finishing what happens when Annie and her father get to town?

_____

_____

_____

_____

_____

There are many different ways to use transitions. They can be used from one paragraph to another; one sentence to another or even within a sentence. They are very important when moving from one chapter to another. Transitions should be brief and inconspicuous in your writing.

 Get your Writing Map 10 **BRIDGES TO TRANSITION** Form from your Travel Kit at the back of this chapter.

Review words and phrases that help make transitions
When Completed store in your Travel Folder

Questions: info@goldenquillpress.com Subject line HTWYB–Map 10

Use this form to add words and phrases you would use to take your characters from one place to another, from one time to another and from one Chapter to another.

ALERT:
**Our Wise Guides Agree:
Transitions are essential to keep your reader from asking—**

Metaphor and Imagery

A metaphor is a figure of speech containing an implied comparison of two things. Often, writers use metaphors to compare feelings to something different, such as an object or action. If you just wanted to show feeling you could write, "She looked sad and began to cry." But when you use a metaphor you can show the feelings as compared to a gray stormy day.

Example: Her face clouded over as the tears rained down her cheeks.
The gloom of the day had settled on her face.
The metaphor combines two ideas that become somewhat the same.

Example: Black velvet curtains of night enfolded the village.
We can visualize the night resembling the curtains as they are closed for the evening

Example: Silver ribbons of water flowed down the mountain.
We visualize water flowing down the mountain in a narrow ribbon.

In the metaphor examples: the storm, curtains, ribbons all add imagery (pictures in the mind) to express the thoughts in a different, but often more powerful manner. Memorable people, places, and experiences, are enhanced by the use of imagery.

Get your Writing Map 10 **METAPHOR, IMAGERY, SIMILE DETAILING** FORM at the back of this chapter.

Decide on one main location - Repeat for additional locations
When Completed store in your Travel Folder

Questions: info@goldenquillpress.com Subject line HTWYB–Map 10

Simile

Simile means likeness or having a resemblance to something.
The man is strong as an elephant.
The man's wrinkled gray skin hung on his bony frame, like an elephant's hide.

You can use metaphors, imagery and similes in your writing to create vivid impressions, that can be interwoven into your story in a subtle manner. They shouldn't appear to be contrived.

Use the form to write your scene adding similes and metaphors to create vivid imagery and use this to add to your scene descriptions.

Turn Right at the Clichés

The word "cliché" means a tired, worn-out, trite expression. Overworked words and phrases can make your writing dull and lacking in freshness and originality.

Change THESE Clichés into better phrases, such as: Music to my ears becomes -- That sounds wonderful!

As luck would have it   _____

Trapped like rats   _____

Cool as a cucumber   _____

Goes without saying   _____

Water over the dam/Water under the bridge _____

See Answers - Next Page

1.The way it turned out 2.Cornered 3.Easy going 4.Words aren't needed 5. No longer important

Stereotyping

An example of stereotyping can be seen in movies where all the good cowboys wear white hats and the bad ones wear black hats.

Fairytales also portray bad witches as ugly with warts on their faces and pointed noses. Good witches are beautiful usually with perfect features and flowing hair. They are portrayed as kind and caring and all knowing.

We may know better, but labeling and prejudging is often easiest, even if it is sometimes inaccurate.

We may have a fixed idea that certain people dress, speak, and act a certain way, and we don't expect a bank robber to be a tiny, gray-haired grandmotherly type--but she could.

The point is; avoid worn-out stereotyping and try to portray your characters in a fresh, original way.

Surprise me with characters that are: different, interesting and filled with unexpected qualities. That makes for a better read!

 Do you have a favorite cliché or one you know you shouldn't always use.

ADD it to our list.
e-mail — info@goldenquillpress.com
Subject line : Cliché s

HOW TO WRITE YOUR BOOK   From an Idea to YOUR PUBLISHED STORY   Your Writing Style

Writing Map 10

TRIP REVIEW

Map Directions

Style Is Your Way Of Expressing Your Ideas & Thoughts; Distinct From Other Writers

Tone Is The Overall Mood You Establish In Your Writing

Metaphors, Imagery & Simile Add Color To Your Writing

Avoid Clichés & Stereotyping

Travel Instructions — Did You?

- ❏ Establish Your Tone
- ❏ Play Metaphor, Simile, & Imagery Game & add to your
- ❏ Build your Bridges to Transitions & add to your

OUR WISE GUIDES
POINT YOU IN THE RIGHT DIRECTION

◀ **NOTE** ▶

Your writing style expresses your visions moving your reader to see, feel and sense not only the magic of your words, but all the meanings they convey.

HOW TO WRITE YOUR BOOK From an Idea to YOUR PUBLISHED STORY   Your Writing Style

Writing Map 10   BRIDGES TO TRANSITIONS   Travel Kit Form

Take your characters from one place to another from one time to another and from one Chapter to another

To add a point: furthermore, in addition, finally, for example, for instance
"In addition to working for the I.S.A you will follow all Dr. Schmidt's orders, no matter what!"

Cause and Effect: because, consequently, as a result, therefore
"As a result of Brad's foolhardy scheme, he will have to face jail time."

Emphasis: above all
Above all Controller must be destroyed.

Spatial: near, far, in front of, beside, beyond, a above, below, to the right, to the left, around, inside, outside
Brad looked around, but only saw one broken vial— the spilled formula was beyond his sight.

Purpose: for this/that reason, for this/that purpose
Controller had to be destroyed or Jonathan would be a zombie forever. For that reason Brad made a deal with Cracko

To contrast: but, however, on the other hand, even though
Even though Evie knew her parents would not be happy she still went to the modeling audition

To compare: in the same way, similarly
Brad never looked at things in the same way as his parents.

Time: now, then, before, after, earlier, later, meanwhile
Jon told Brad; earlier that night he gave into temptation. He begged Sheila for more candies.

To summarize: in summary, in conclusion, to sum up
"In conclusion, Dr. Schmidt, we don't know how to destroy Controller."

Take your characters from one place to another from one time to another and from one Chapter to another

_____
_____
_____
_____
_____
_____
_____
_____
_____
_____
_____
_____
_____
_____
_____
_____
_____
_____
_____
_____
_____
_____
_____
_____
_____
_____
_____
_____
_____
_____
_____

HOW TO WRITE YOUR BOOK   From an Idea to YOUR PUBLISHED STORY   Your Writing Style

Writing Map 10   METAPHOR, IMAGERY, SIMILE   Travel Kit Form

METAPHOR, IMAGERY SIMILE Example:

The rain was pounding on her car's hood, but Evie didn't seem to notice. Through water drenched eyes all she could see was Rick. She'd never met anyone who knocked her off her feet the way he did. He was like a diamond in the rough; trying to hid all the facets of his personality.

As she watched him fixing her car, her heart seemed to leap out of her chest like the thunder that was blasting in the distance.

The lightening illuminated his face and once again she saw that little boy look. Everyone said he was "bad," but she could see beneath that facade to the depths of his soul. She hoped someday he'd see her that way: through the eyes of love.

Write your scene adding similes and metaphors to create vivid imagery. Use to add to your scene descriptions.
_____
_____
_____
_____
_____
_____
_____
_____
_____
_____
_____
_____
_____
_____
_____
_____
_____
_____
_____
_____
_____
_____
_____
_____
_____
_____
_____
_____
_____
_____

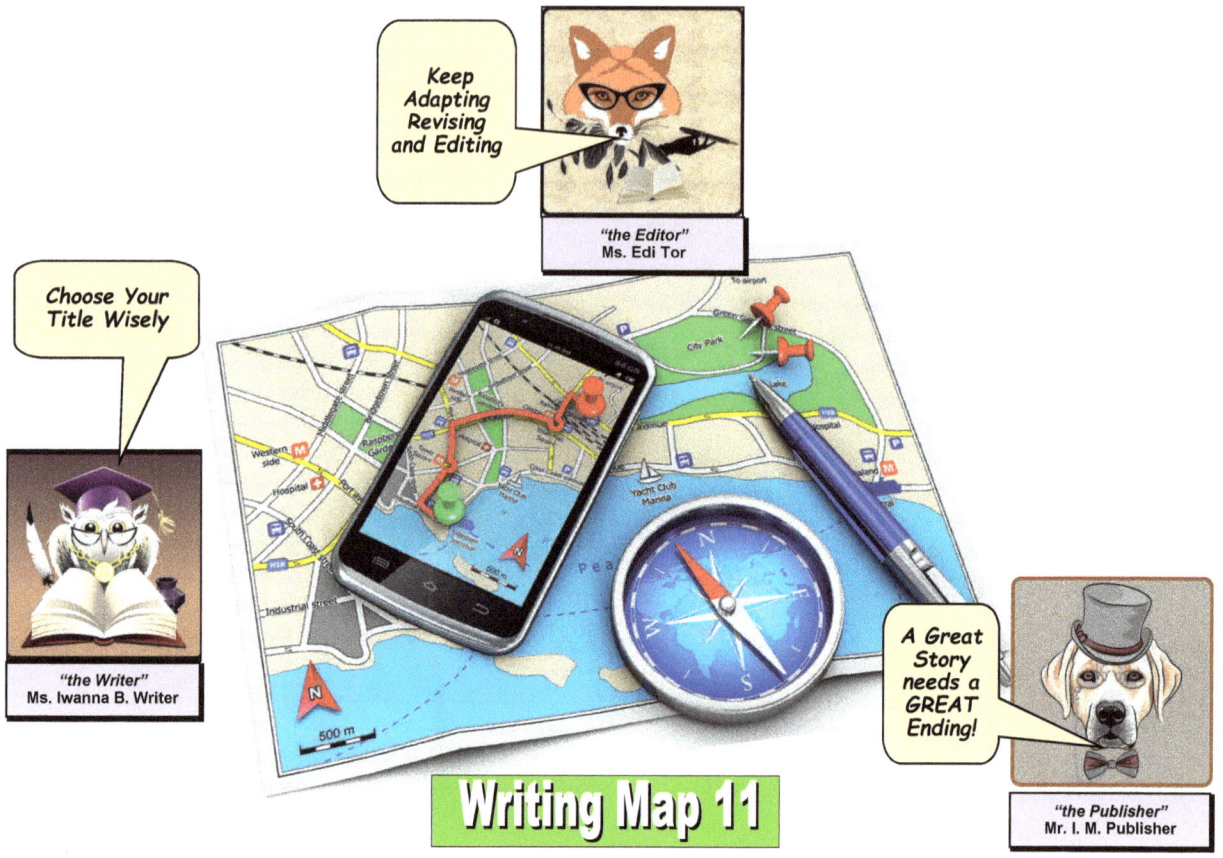

FINISHING WITH A FLAIR

Now that your story has all the elements that best sellers are made of, you want to be sure you give the same attention to the ending. Many times when a writer gets to this point, they rush to get finished. Taking time to plot out the ending will prove worthwhile; a great ending will leave your readers panting for more. One of the key elements to a great ending is for the story to come full circle. Full circle means: you have tied up all the loose ends, revealed all the details that you withheld along the way, and as your readers turn to the last page you leave them wishing for more.

Just like hooking your readers in the beginning and keeping them interested all the way through; the ending is pivotal. There are many possibilities for ways to create a great ending and here are just a few: Surprise, Poetic, Summary.

Many Roads lead to a Successful Ending

As with the rest of your story, your style and story line has been a determining factor and your ending is no different. How you end your book should follow the same pattern as how you have written the book—but this is the time when you can get very creative. Your beginning hook got your reader to continue reading -- now take advantage of the chance to WOW your reader one last time! It's important. Endings do not have to be long and drawn out—but they must be fantastic.

Surprise Ending: You've been leading the reader along and the reader expects a certain ending—but you change direction and pull off the unexpected.

Poetic Ending: All's well that ends well. This is a popular way to end a book— and it generally satisfies the reader. Many readers want books to end on a "happy note."

Summation Ending: The story summation, usually by a main character reiterating the events that led to that point.

Continuation Ending. This ending sets your book up for a sequel — and leaves the reader with a new situation, or a question that's still hanging when the book ends —usually to be resolved in the next book.

Alert— Alert: Our Wise Guides Note:

Some endings may even have a little of all the formulas, just remember the best endings are ones that leave the reader satisfied. But if you've written a book 300 pages in length; summing up the whole book in a page or two seems a bit abrupt.

Don't Let Your Readers Down At The End!
Nothing is worse for a reader than to have spent their time with your entire story, only to be let down and disappointed at the end!

 Get your Writing Map 11 **END DETAILING** Form from your Travel Kit at the back of this chapter

When Completed store in your Travel Folder

Questions: info@goldenquillpress.com Subject line HTWYB–Map 11

Decide on your ending style and write your ending. You may want to try out a few possibilities before you decide on the final one.

Finally! You've finished a First Draft — Celebrate!!! Next, sit down and then, CONGRATULATE yourself. This is a BIG STEP. As soon as you've enjoyed the moment, shared it with family and friends — reveled in your success, and had a good nights sleep, then we can continue on the last leg of the journey.

Onto the Next Road

TITLE: Let's go back to your original title. Many times when we finish a story the original title may still be fantastic -- but it may also be very wrong. You'll need to be even more objective at this time.

A Word About Titles

   The title of your book is important because it's what your reader sees first. Many readers judge a book by its title and decide whether they want to take the book off the shelf. Now that you know, make sure your Title takes advantage of "the first chance to make a good impression," and choose your title carefully.

 Think of your favorite book — movie, TV show – then change the Title – If the only information you had was a Title — would you still choose it. That's how important a Title can be!

Play the Title Game: When we change the following Titles, see how it affects you.

Gone With the Wind	to	A Plantation in the South
Carrie	to	Strange Girl at the Prom
Star Trek	to	Journey through the Solar Systems
The Wizard of Oz	to	Dreams of Far Away Places

Which would you choose?

   The same analysis is needed with your Title. Here are a few tips to keep in mind. The title should tell what the book is about in an eye-catching way. But remember Titles shouldn't divulge Too Much! Some Titles promise adventure while others a hint of romance, but Titles can entice readers in such a way that they can't wait to read that book.
   Study book titles to see how they tie in with the contents and message of a book. Look at the book cover. What does it convey? Study both front and back covers to see how the written material and cover design tie in with the title. Sometimes a title like, "Gone with the Wind," or our book, "Code 47 to BREV Force," doesn't mean anything to a reader. However, the title takes on meaning and when combined with the cover design conveys the message of the book.
   Note how some books have a subtitle: Sometimes when a title is unclear, a subtitle is used. Sub-titles can also be further inducement to the reader:
   "The Legend of Black Sandy Beach - Survival on a Deserted Island"
   "Rags To Riches -- The Stock Market Killing"
   "TELL IT TO THE FUTURE-- Have I Got A Story For You…"

Some questions to ask about your title: Does your book have a direct promise? "Helpful Hints to Lose Weight Fast" Note: Be Sure Your Book Doesn't Promise Something It Doesn't Deliver!

Does the title identify with your story? "Justice is Blind" If your story has nothing to do with fairness, a trial or something in that category – it may be a great Title, but not for your book.

Our Wise Guides Suggest:
If you' re looking to sell your story and the Editor and Publisher suggest a Title change — remember they have experience with books that sell — and one's that don't!

Get your Writing Map 11 **TITLE DETAILING** Form from your Travel Kit at the back of this chapter

When Completed store in your Travel Folder

Questions: info@goldenquillpress.com Subject line HTWYB–Map 11

First skim through your first draft and try to identify what elements would make the title fit your story. Jot them down. Write your original Title and see if the elements of your story lead to that Title or if a better Title surfaces. You can also ask family and friends, especially those who buy books, or are library junkies.

EDITING-REVISING

The Road to the Final Manuscript

Now that you've completed your first draft, we can get back on the highway that will lead to your final manuscript. This may seem like a long and windy road, and you may be asking yourself why you need to take that road — the answer is simple — all your hard work got your ideas down on paper—now your story needs to be perfected. You need to take on this part of your journey with the same planning and enthusiasm as the previous parts of your trip. If you do, you'll find this last leg of the journey to be very exciting…and thrilling as you realize how close you are to the finished story.

During this part of your journey Mrs. Edi Tor and Mr. I. M. Publisher, will be your navigators. In order to properly edit and revise your draft you'll need to be very objective, and leave your ego at the door. You may feel every word you've written, is a gem; every thought incredible and every sentence and character necessary -- but "it ain't necessarily so!" If you want to make your journey effective, you need to stop and carefully analyze what you've written.

If you can't do that, don't beat yourself up — everyone needs a travel agent at some time. That is why there are professional editors.

For our purposes let's assume you are raring to go and have pointed your vehicle in the right direction -- here's your road map through this hilly terrain. Answer these questions as you begin to read your first draft aloud. Try to listen as the passenger, rather than the driver. This reading is not for grammar and spelling mistakes, it's a rethinking of all aspects of your story.

Take out your Travel Folder and refer back to ALL your Writing Plan Detailing Forms. As you read your first draft, look back to be sure you've used all the important information and that you didn't mix up character details. Decide what improvements you can make to turn your first draft into your edited manuscript.

DRAFT TO MANUSCRIPT CHECK LIST:

- ☐ <u>Does your story have an interesting beginning?</u>
  - ☐ Are the first 10 pages slow or fast paced
  - ☐ Does the story get started in those first 10 pages
  - ☐ What has been introduced to make the reader want to turn to the next page
  - ☐ Is there an easily recognizable lead or a hook that will hold your reader's interest
  - ☐ Is the hook unique (not usual or expected)
  - ☐ Is the hook strong enough to keep the reader turning pages
  - ☐ Does the hook appear in the first few pages

- ☐ <u>Are your characters dynamic?</u>
  - ☐ Do they cause the reader to root for them or hate them
  - ☐ Are they realistic
  - ☐ Do they each have a goal or reason for being in the story
  - ☐ Does the dialogue move the story along
  - ☐ Do your characters express what is happening by dialogue, as well as by their actions
  - ☐ Do the character descriptions bring to mind a visual picture

- ☐ <u>Is the time and place clear and interesting?</u>
  - ☐ Is the main setting memorable
  - ☐ Does the place and time fit with your story and work well for the story

- ☐ <u>Has the story line included problems that need to be solved?</u>
  - ☐ Were the problems clearly explained so the reader could follow the flow
  - ☐ Before the end of the story were all the problems and conflicts resolved

- ☐ <u>Were all the loose ends tied up so the reader will be satisfied?</u>
  - ☐ Has every characters situation been explained and wrapped up by the end of the story

HOW TO WRITE YOUR BOOK   From an Idea to YOUR PUBLISHED STORY   Finishing With A Flair

Now really step back – and think about the questions Our Wise Guides are asking

 Do you Want To Test Drive Your Manuscript ?
email: info@goldenquillpress.com
Subject line: Writer's Evaluation

Alert— Alert: Our Wise Guides Strongly Suggest:

DON"T JUST DO AS WE SAY—DO AS WE DO!

Before you send your work to a publisher or editor — do what we do —

Have a Professional (not a friend) look at your work.

 FOR details about professional editing check out
our **website** at: www.goldenquillpress.com
Or **email**: info@goldenquillpress.com
Subject line: Editing

HOW TO WRITE YOUR BOOK   From an Idea to YOUR PUBLISHED STORY   Finishing With A Flair

TRIP REVIEW

Map Directions

Title Is The Judge That Gets Your Book Off The Shelf

Endings Are As Important As Beginnings

Celebrate Finishing The First Draft

Revise and Edit As If You Were Reading The Book For The First Time

Travel Instructions — Did You?

- ❑ Devise a Great Ending and add to your
- ❑ Play the Title Game and add to your
- ❑ Use your Detailing Forms to help you Revise and Edit

OUR WISE GUIDES
POINT YOU IN THE RIGHT DIRECTION

"A Wise Old, Young Owl" What a GREAT Title

Do What the FOX SAYS! Revise & Edit until your story is a Howling Success

A Great Ending gets my tail wagging!

◀ **NOTE** ▶

Remember the reader can't get into your head – and, you can't always assume what a reader knows – or understands --

HOW TO WRITE YOUR BOOK   From an Idea to YOUR PUBLISHED STORY   Finishing With A Flair

Writing Map 11 — ENDING DETAILING — Travel Kit Form

Summation Ending

The BREV Force hung up their costumes after the press conference and returned to their normal lives. Brian enrolled in Norton University and Ginger helped him get into the routine of college life. He also got a job as a computer specialist with the management company at Compustock Mall. Brian still thought about Robin, but never mentioned her to anyone.

Brad was trying to balance school, work and Francoise who was the only girl he was dating.

Evie was happier than ever. Her job as a fashion designer apprentice got her a first chance to design a new wedding collection, under her name, *"designs by eve-lyn!"*

Martin and Vivian returned to their research work for National Security and enjoyed new baby, Marcella.

Remy now headed up the International Alliance of Scientists and was seated in his new office at their headquarters in Geneva. He was beginning to get acclimated to his new position and into a routine of commuting back and forth, by teleportation to his new home in Island Falls.

Having arrived early that morning, Remy waited while his holographic secretary reported the day's schedule and began processing the daily reports which were coming in from all over the world..

While the Rhapsody played on the Symphonic speaker System, in the background Remy relaxed with his morning coffee before getting to the work at hand. He had missed seeing his daughter Francoise that morning before he left and was eagerly awaiting a "good morning" e-mail. He clicked on his inbox in hopes of finding her friendly smile.

The End

(NOTE: This final paragraph can also make the ending a Continuation...hopefully for your BEST SELLING SEQUEL!)

Your Ending Choice: _____

Writing Map 11 — TITLE DETAILING — Travel Kit Form

HOW TO WRITE YOUR BOOK From an Idea to YOUR PUBLISHED STORY   Finishing With A Flair

Original title: Teen Force

Elements:
  Teenager become superheroes Force against computer virus
  Respond to Code to become super heroes
  Names equals combination of their names
  B = Br ad and Br ian
  R = r and Remy
  E = Ev ie
  V = v and Vivian
  47 =is numeric value of names

Possible Titles:
  Teens against Computer Virus Becoming Super Heroes

Words that might form a title —
 Teen , Super, heroes, Force, computer, virus, Code, Names, BREV, 47

Possible New Title
  Code 47 to BREV Force

Compare to your original
  Teen Force

Which do you believe is a better title?

  Code 47 to BREV Force

(when you go through your draft for editing and revising -- keep this Title in mind, but be open to the possibility of another Title jumping out at you).

HOW TO WRITE YOUR BOOK From an Idea to YOUR PUBLISHED STORY   Take Your Story To Market

TAKE YOUR STORY TO MARKET

Now that we have a finished manuscript we're almost at the end of our journey. You've traveled many roads to get here and now you need to make the most of your progress. With so many possibilities we need to first decide the right direction to take. But before we can do that we need to dress the part.

Manuscript Preparation Checklist

This is similar to the draft checklist, but now we're adding the finishing touches. When preparing your manuscript, stick to the basics. The Sample Forms on the next few pages will help you understand proper format. On the Cover Page in the right hand corner you need to indicate the word count. If you work with a computer go to: Tools, then click on word count. This box will come up:>>>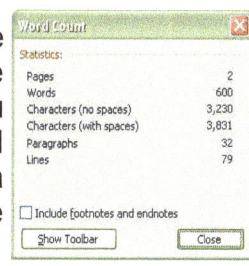

If you don't have a computer, you'll need to use the old fashioned method - COUNT! Estimate by counting number of words across the page, multiplied by number of lines down. Ex::10 words across x 25 lines = 250 words per page. Multiply by the number of pages to get an approximate number of words. Approximate is usually close enough, but the computer will give you an exact number. **Note: When revising your work—cutting or adding copy—always re-check your word count.**

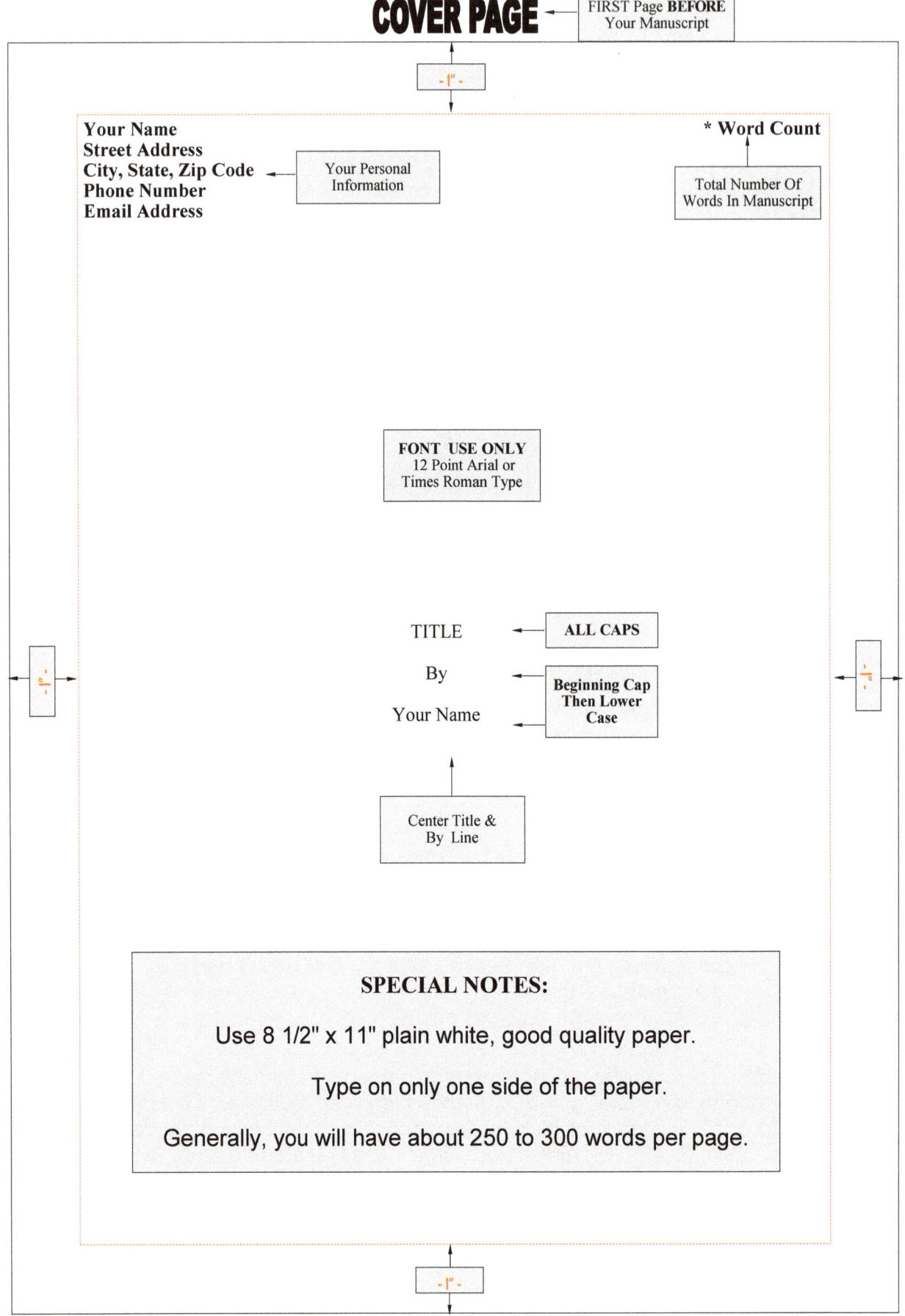

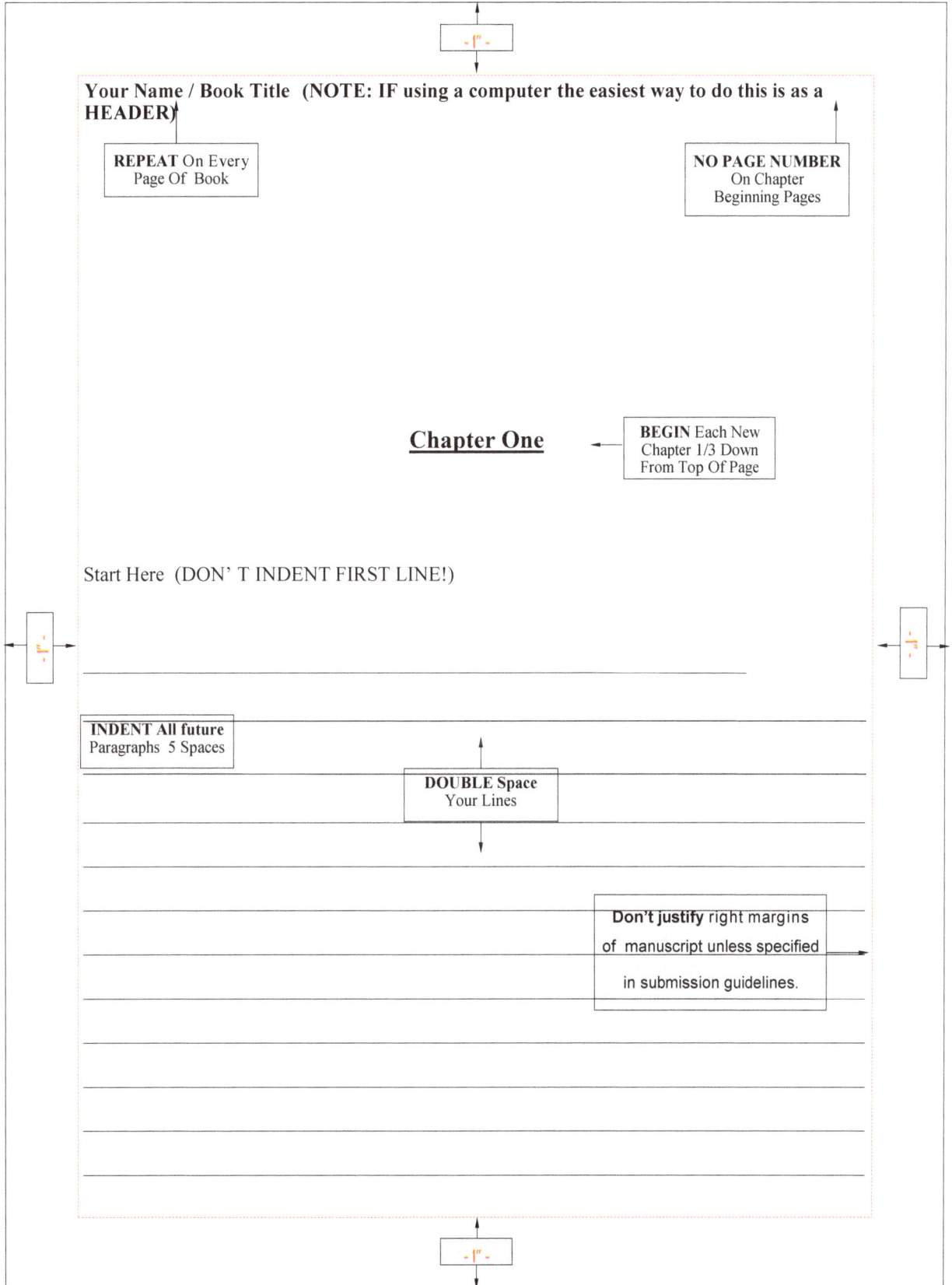

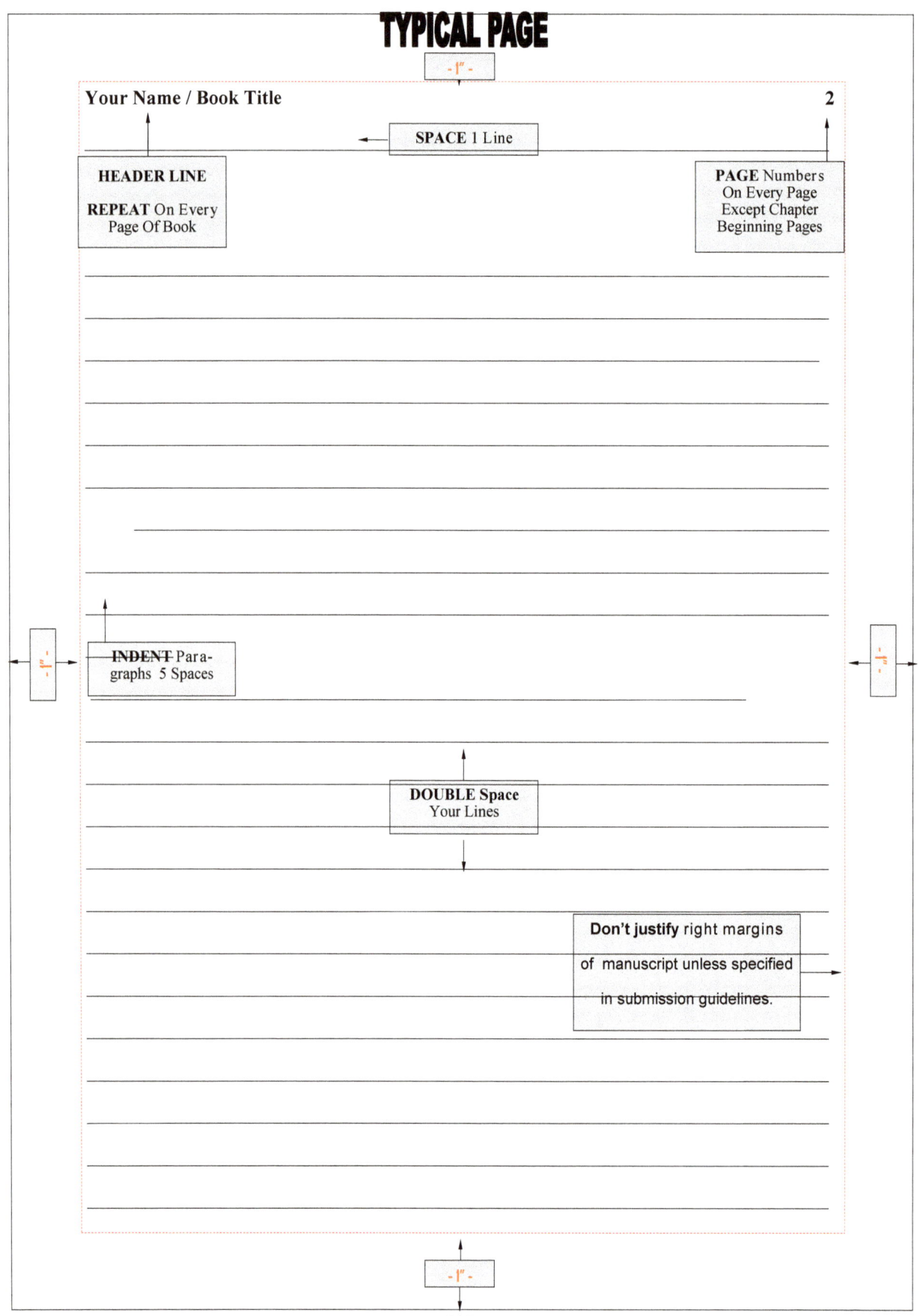

Just Along for the Ride

If you've written your story just for yourself, your family and friends or to leave for future generations, then this is the end of your road. You Did IT! You now have a FINISHED MANUSCRIPT, – and We Are VERY PROUD of YOU! Even if your work was just for yourself, we suggest you consider making copies and giving them to those who'll appreciate your efforts and enjoy the fruits of your labors.

We also hope since you've worked so hard, you might now consider publishing, as an option. Even if you have no intention of selling to bookstores, you may want your story converted into a conventional book. POD or Print on Demand services will print just 1, or more books). If this journey has given you the slightest urge, please, get back on the road with us and continue the journey to that end.

Admiring the Scenery on Genré Highway

Establishing your Genré means to decide on the category (Genré) for your writing: If you're not sure what category is right, visit your local library or bookstore and check other books in the genre you believe is similar to yours. By a process of elimination you should be able to correctly identify your genre. — Here's a list of some choices:

Action	Horror
Adventure	Mainstream
Biographical	Mystery
Children	Romance
Contemporary	Science-Fiction
Crime	Suspense
Fantasy	Western
Historical	Young Adult

While browsing amongst the books, note that non-fiction covers a wide selection of categories. How to books, Cook books, and Business related books are just a few.

Now that we know which genré your story fits into, next we need to see whose publishing what you're writing. There are many good tools on the market to help you familiarize yourself with the publishing industry. Writer's Market and Literary Marketplace are two sources for searching out what publisher's are looking for and their requirements. Just keep in mind, these reference sources are published annually and information may be out of date. Publishers Weekly is another important resource which can be found at most libraries. It's chock full of who's publishing what, trends, reviews and additional information.

Publisher's web sites have also become very informative. Many publisher's have internet sites that include: books they've published, their imprints, and some even include submission requirements and e-mail addresses for editors.

It's also acceptable to call publishing houses and request guidelines, or verify editor's names and positions. Another way to get the information is to scan the shelves of libraries and bookstores to find books similar to yours. Check out who published them. Many times just by flipping through the front and back you may find an acknowledgement or thank you with the editor's name.

Driving to your Genré

The book business is genré driven so first be sure the publisher you have chosen to send your work to publishes in your genré. Suppose your novel is science fiction and you find this listing:

> Silver Lane an imprint (division) of Meredith House.
> Silver Lane--Currently publishing 9 books a year;
> 6 Science Fiction and 3 Historical Non-Fiction.
> First time novelists accepted. Bob Bara; Editor-in-Chief,
> Mary Meed; Science Fiction Editor, George Gee;
> Historical Editor.
> We respond within 3 months. (555-555-5555)
> 330 Next St., New Book, VA 00000

The Editor-in-Chief is rarely the first to read a new manuscript, and a senior editor is always better to approach then a junior

Major Publishers usually have many imprints—be sure you contact the one that's right for your book

You should send to the science fiction (genré) editor, Mary Meed. If the listing doesn't indicate what to send, you should check the internet or call and ask for guidelines.

Alert, Alert: Our Experts Agree:

NEVER SEND
your manuscript to a publisher whose listing states,
"we do not accept unsolicited manuscripts"
This phrase, "Unsolicited manuscripts," is common in the publishing industry.
Basically it means, don't call us, we'll call you!

Another phrase to be aware of is: **"DO NOT ACCEPT MULTIPLE SUBMISSIONS," or "SIMULTANEOUS SUBMISSIONS."** If that's the case only send your work to one publisher at a time.

OUR GUIDES ADVISE:
If this phrase is in the guidelines decide which publisher you believe is your best chance and only send the requested materials to that publisher. If you receive a rejection, or no response from that publisher, after the time they state they'll respond, then you are free to send to others.

Remember also, if a listing states, "agented submissions only" you can only submit through an agent!

All Dressed Up with Somewhere to Go -- Manuscript Submission

Now that you know your genré and which publisher might be interested in your type of work, you're ready to begin the task of marketing. We've met many writers who don't have a clue about this part of the process: marketing their work. They don't read all the guidelines, or ignore them, thinking, "my book is just what that editor is looking for." Or, they just send out manuscripts to publishers at random, only to have their hopes dashed by rejection after rejection. Also, because they don't understand the publishers requirements, they send the full manuscript, instead of what the publisher asked for. Some writers don't include a SASE (self-addressed stamped envelope, or manuscript box) and don't receive their manuscript back—only a letter). This is VERY COSTLY and a BIG WASTE OF TIME!

Our Experts Agree:

DON"T SEND YOUR MANUSCRIPT
unless it says to do so in the submission guidelines.

When you do send your work, be sure to include a cover letter with your return address and phone number. Also include materials and adequate postage for the manuscript's return. Many first time writers make the mistake of only sending their manuscripts to the most successful larger publishers and ignore the smaller houses. Our Experts suggest you may find it easier to market to a small house, but you should still research both small and large publishing firms.

Other Avenues to Market First

If you want to get your name out there before you approach agents or publishers, try essays and short stories for magazines and local newspapers. Study the contents of a variety of publications and look for trends. Generally, magazine editors need stories and articles months in advance and will expect you to follow specific guidelines.

The masthead in magazines will list the editors and their titles.
- Helen Hill - Food Editor
- Steven Chase - Education
- Myra Morton - Garden Editor
- Peter Thomas - Travel

In order to correctly market a short story or article you must obtain guidelines and be sure the finished work is sent to the proper editor.

Take the Right Manuscript Submission Exit

Before sending anything, ascertain exactly what the publisher wants. Many publishers require a query* or synopsis* before seeing the entire manuscript. (*see more information on next page). Sometimes they may also want to see the first three chapters. Different publishers have different submission requirements so to save time; find out first!

Even a great story idea can be rejected if the Query doesn't do it justice

Drive one block and turn on Query Street

When you're ready to turn in the direction of publishers and agents, you may need to write a query. To query means to "ask," and in this case you're asking a publisher to consider your work. You hope their interest will be piqued enough by your fantastic query to want to see more. This letter of inquiry requires your best thinking and writing. This is your opportunity to sell yourself and your book.
[The query letter should be written as a sales pitch, or a movie trailer; summing up your book in no more than one exciting page. Generally you don't need a separate cover letter. Be sure you include all the best elements of your story — hero, villains, conflict, resolution and leave the editor with a teaser. Most importantly show the editor your style of writing. Don't forget to check spelling and grammar check.

Write that Exciting Query that reads like the best introduction or back cover for your book:

Points to Include:
- ❑ Opening sentence or paragraph "Hook"
- ❑ Fantastic story Premise
- ❑ A quote or paragraph that really sells your idea
- ❑ Identify your target reader
- ❑ What makes this story similar to other best selling novels, or different enough to be a crowd pleaser
- ❑ Always include something about yourself and mention previous writing that shows your ability. (note: if you're a first time novelist and don't have any other writing credit, tell why you're qualified to write this book)
- ❑ Be sure to thank the editor for his or her time
- ❑ Include a SASE (self addressed stamped envelope)

Be sure you have the right editor's name and that it's spelled Correctly!

Don't send a completed manuscript unless the editor asks for it. Also check the guidelines to see whether the editor wants you to send any chapters or other materials along with the query.

SEE SAMPLE QUERY LETTER ON NEXT PAGE

SAMPLE QUERY LETTER

Write a Query for Your Book. Here's an sample to follow:

15 Willow Sweep Rd
Scotts land, BB 22222

July 15, 2016

Children's Editions
34 Bookland Ave. 16th Floor
New Market, NN 001111
Attention: Marian Rusen, Sr. Editor

Dear Ms. Rusen:

"The Adventures of the We Clan" brilliantly unfolds for children 5-8 years of age, as they experience what it's like to be different and what standing up for themselves means. The We Clan gives us a portrayal of characters that will delight children with their uniqueness. The Clan will also help children have a better understanding of relationships, being different in our world, its animals and other species.

This adventure/fantasy takes children into the imaginary world of these "Smurf" size people who live in a cave. They have strong moral views and family values that are nurtured in a very structured society. Problems occur when a normal size man, who seems like a giant to them, enters their cave and steals a treasured harp they use in all their celebrations. Horrendous unhappiness befalls the We Clan who now must challenge the "Giant" for their possession. The reader experiences many adventures on their escapade to retrieve the harp and enjoys a touching moment as they are befriended by neighboring animals. With the help of these new found friends, they storm the Giant's Castle; find the harp and barely escape the Giant's fury. They emerge victorious and return home with the animals to celebrate

To test market this idea I went to a local school and the response was overwhelming. Not only did the story keep and hold the children's attention, they were so excited they couldn't wait to hear how the story would end. They voted for their favorite characters, booed the Giant and picked their favorite cover.

Strong characters, imaginative experiences and life lessons give this story the type of possibilities for success that your company has achieved with the H. Possem Series. I am sure you will love the We Clan and clamor to see more . The first three chapters of the manuscript are enclosed as per your submission guidelines and a SASE for return of materials. Thank you for your time and consideration.

Sincerely,

Barbara Bee
Encl:

PREPARING TO SEND!

An editor and publisher were once heard to say:

So keep it simple and properly prepared and you'll get started on the right road.

Note:
Many un-agented manuscripts wind up in a "Slush pile" and usually a junior editor may glance at the work, only to send a rejection. There are just too many submissions and too few editors. Your best bet to get to anyone of real importance is to present a great idea, that fits the publishers list, and is properly prepared to wow the editor and publisher. It does happen!

Should You E-mail Queries?

It's best to find out if e-mail is accepted. If so, go for it. Be sure to use the format they request .doc or .pdf etc. and send only what they request. If not, go the usual postal letter route.

 If you would like professional assistance in preparing, or editing your query you can **email:** info@goldenquillpress.com Subject line: Query Assistance

 Get your Writing Map 12 **TRACKING DETAIL** Form
from your Travel Kit at the back of this chapter

When Completed store in your Travel Folder

Questions: info@goldenquillpress.com Subject line HTWYB–Map 12

P.S. The Map 12 Tracking Form can also be used for
Synopsis, Proposals and Manuscripts.

Synopsis Road

Sometimes an editor will want a synopsis. This is a complete outline of your book. They may want it chapter by chapter or just the major events. Length also can vary from one or two pages to 10 plus; double-spaced. But the most important thing for you to know is a synopsis needs to read like a story outline and yet be as interesting and exciting as the book itself. It must show your writing style. The synopsis is always written: in present tense, third person and should weave your story from one sentence to the next. Tell all the points: don't hint at or imply and be sure to include: the Hook, beginning middle, climax and end. Keep dialogue to the barest minimum, if at all. A good synopsis should be able to sell you and your story, so don't forget to check for grammar and spelling errors.

 If you would like professional assistance in preparing, or editing your synopsis **email:** info@goldenquillpress.com Subject line: Assistance Synopsis

Detailing the Road of Proposals:

Proposals are in-depth analysis of your book. They are generally required for non-fiction. A Proposal should include: marketing and sales projections, competitive works, author's information and promotional skills, table of contents, chapter by chapter outline, sample chapters and synopsis. Proposals are very detailed. We recommend getting complete guidelines and looking at sample proposals before even attempting this task.

 If you would like professional assistance in preparing, or editing your proposal you can **email:** info@goldenquillpress.com Subject line: Assistance Proposal

Sending your work to Publishers

A word about sending your work to publishers. Many times we've heard first time novelists concern about someone stealing story ideas. Usually publishers have heard every type of idea concept at one time or another and most stories are just different versions of a similar theme. Of course it could happen, so we can not give you a guarantee. All we can say is, if you're really concerned, mail a copy of your manuscript to yourself and do not open it. The United States Postal date stamp proves the date you sent the finished work to yourself. That may at least give you some peace of mind.

We are also asked about copyright. Most first time authors feel they must have their work copy written. This is also not necessary. Under U.S. copyright laws the author is the owner of all rights to their literary work. When your book is published official copyright will be obtained for you as the author.

**Alert – Alert Our Experts Suggest
Always Keep A Copy of Whatever You Send
For your Own Records!**

Telephoning Editors

When your query is being considered be aware of the timeline given and don't telephone before a reasonable amount of time. If the guidelines indicate 3 months, wait the full amount of time and add two weeks before calling, but only if guidelines say you can call.

The Billboard Says, "The Editor wants to read YOUR entire Manuscript!"

An editor's job is to obtain the most marketable materials possible, so if they want to see your manuscript you're on the right road. Be sure you send a properly prepared manuscript,(see our guidelines earlier in this chapter). Remember no rubber bands, paper clips — fancy folders, just loose in a manuscript box. (These can be gotten at stationary or office supply stores). Some writers want to send a picture of what their cover should look like, the back cover and a list of people they want to thank etc. Again we remind you, do not send anything but the manuscript, and be sure to enclose a SASE (self addressed stamped envelope, or box with enough postage) if you want your work returned. Always enclose a cover letter reminding the editor you were asked to send the manuscript.

When you start to send out queries and manuscripts keep a log of dates and editor's names. This will help you track the manuscript dates sent, returned and the results. This form will also help you know which editors not to resend. Sometimes editors may change or there may be two editors in the same division — so keep your records accurate. Also, keep any notes or letters of rejection. Be sure to check publisher's listings often. Many times publishers might be looking for exactly what you have 6 months down the line, or editors change and the new one may be interested in your work.

Hard Copy or Disk

When an editor wants to see your entire manuscript and requests both hard copy (on paper) and disk, (computer disk) be sure you use a program that is compatible with what they're requesting. Inquire if you are not sure.

Understanding the Agent's Role

If you decide the direct road to the publisher is blocked or closed to you, an agent may be another answer. Getting an agent can be as difficult as finding a publisher. Use the same resources to get a list of agent's names. Then do your research and check each agent's background to be sure that agent works with your genré and has sold work to publishers. Do this before contacting them. There are many fine agents, but unfortunately, there are some so called "agents" who are just looking for a way to make money off a desperate writer and may not be legitimate. Remember to be an agent, all you have to do is say, "I'm an agent!" Also, if an agent asks for money be on the alert. There are associations and guilds that can advise you if this is a fair practice. Just do your homework and you'll be fine!

A good agent works for you and with you to get the best deal for your book. An agent finds the right publisher and then negotiates the contract and legal aspects regarding your work.

When you're looking for an agent, keep in mind that many may not accept your type of writing or take on first time authors

If you take the Wrong Turn and your Work is Rejected?

Authors in our workshops have told us they could paper walls with the rejection letters they've received, before getting that all-important "yes." They've also confirmed our belief that if you have a great story, that is well written; you'll eventually find the right match: the right publisher.

Getting a rejection note or letter should not be taken personally. The editor or agent may not accept your book for many reasons other than it wasn't good: another book on the same topic may be in the works, the publisher can't take anything else on, or the budget is too tight. Another point to be aware of is that the publishing house may only publish a specific number of certain types of books during their budget year. They may like your book, but have no money for its purchase, or have reached their quota for that type of book.

Be happy if an editor or agent takes time to give you a few words of encouragement. You may be advised to try another publisher. Do it! Do it over and over, and keep learning with each submission. Authors try for years to get published. Many famous authors experienced numerous rejections including the now famous author of Harry Potter, J. K. Rowling, and the best selling author Stephen King. They kept banging on doors until they got their first break — so you'll be in good company. Like them, you must believe in your story: your dream. Never give up until you've exhausted every avenue   Keep your rejection letters; not to paper a wall, but to remind you to be persistent, and remember how many famous authors were once just like you; first-time novelist.

Another Highway To Consider

Sometimes it's hard to be objective about your work. Friends and family want to cheer you on but may not be the best critic. You may want to seek professional advice. Published authors, editors and publishers can guide you regarding your work. You might want to get a professional opinion or an evaluation. You can do this before you begin sending to publishers or after you've received rejections

For more information about evaluations or consultations visit our website at:

   www.goldenquillpress.com or **email:** info@goldenquillpress.com

When Your Work Is Accepted

Don't give up movie and TV rights that might be worth more $$$ than you'll make on the book

Of course if your story isn't suited for movies or TV, then get the best book deal possible

When your work is accepted, if you don't have an agent, it may be advisable to seek legal counsel. Even though most contracts are standard — you may be able to negotiate for rights you didn't even know you have. You should always read any legal papers carefully before signing and ask questions when something isn't clear. Advances and royalty percentages will be negotiated and then a final contract will be drawn up listing your rights and the rights you have given to the publisher. If there're rights you want to keep, you need be sure you haven't negotiated those rights away, and have a full understanding of what is stated in the final contract.

   **Our Experts Agree:** A Literary Attorney Should Be Consulted When Your Work is Accepted By a Publisher

Once you begin to work with a publisher you may be assigned an editor, and you may be asked to rewrite, make changes, delete or add copy. The editor's job is to guide you to make your work more marketable. Editors are always pleased when a manuscript is so well written that it needs little or no revisions. The copy editor will check your grammar, punctuation, spelling and more. A smart author will make the copy editor's job easy by doing a line by line editing before submitting the manuscript. You may also be required to submit all your editing changes by a certain date. Your contract may detail dates for revisions and if you don't comply, your publisher may have the right to ask for the return of any advance paid to you, or hold up other money. Therefore, it's extremely important that you adhere to those dates. Also be aware that if you want something changed, it must be approved before that final date. Publishers invest a great deal of money, time and personnel in your work and have a set budget with projected dates for galley's, reviews and marketing. Pre-publication and actual publication dates and tours are set up in advance. Any delays can change the whole time-table and be very costly.

Many book deals have penalties if work is not delivered on time

Getting on the Road to Publishing

When your work is accepted, you should set up a bookkeeping system to record income from any advance and royalties. All your expenses related to writing and publishing your book should be kept and recorded for tax purposes.

   **Our Experts Agree:** A tax specialist should be consulted to help you understand the process and advise you regarding your taxes.

Your Star Walk of Fame

Publishers expect you to do your part to help sell your book. Most publishers want to know you better so they can properly promote your book. Some questions you may be asked are:

- ☐ Are you willing to do book signings and tour?
- ☐ Do you have public speaking experience?
- ☐ Would you be able to address audiences at organizations, schools, colleges, and businesses?
- ☐ Would you be able to handle interviews with magazines, newspapers, television or radio?
- ☐ Do you know your competitors?
- ☐ Have you looked at the features and benefits of your book as compared to others?
- ☐ Why is your book better?

To sum it up, you're expected to look, act, and speak the part of the successful author when in the public eye. This doesn't mean all authors travel, appear on TV or address live audiences. The nature of your work helps the publisher determine how to promote and publicize your book. The point is, the more you can offer the publisher in promoting your work; the better.

Other Avenues of Publication:

Self-Publishing

A number of best-selling books by famous authors have been self-published. Some of these have later been picked up by major publishers or have become motion pictures. If you want to keep full control of your work and have the time, energy, money, and contacts, you might prefer self-publishing where all the decisions are yours.

Self-publishing has advantages and disadvantages to consider and is not necessarily for everyone. You need to be aware that unless you have contacts and marketing know-how, your sales may be limited. Not being familiar with publishing: your costs may be higher, you may order more books than you need, or are able to sell. You have to wear many hats: author, publisher, marketer, promoter, shipper, etc. You may not be able to devote the time and needed resources to make your book a success. Again, it's good business to get all the information you can from more than one source before considering self-publishing. Read a few books on the subject, talk to others who have self-published, and be ready to invest a little more than pocket money.

Self- Publishing On–Line

Many first time or even popular authors are using the vast resources of the internet to publish their work on-line.

As in days of old there are still Vanity Publisher's, but we prefer to concentrate on the new sources of internet publishers, such as Amazon's CreateSpace, LuLu, and IngramSpark, just to name a few.

These sites will offer different ideas and pricing for Print on Demand. With Print on Demand you do not pay for a set number of books to be printed they are offered on the internet and when purchased you receive a prearranged amount for the sale of that book, almost like a commission. You have no print run cost or worries about storing and eventually selling thousands of books; but you may not make as much on each book, so volume will help. Also it is important to note that there are so many books on the internet currently we do not even want to give you a number as it changes that quickly, however, if you have a good sense of the internet and can maneuver your way through social media, this may be the way for you.

E-Book Publishing Only

Another technique for authors is ebook publishing. This has become so popular that everywhere you turn there are e-books for FREE and for Sale. Making your book into an e-book may actually be the easy part. There are sites all over the internet just waiting to help you. Amazon offer's their Kindle/KDP program, Ingram Spark, LuLu and so many more. Just do a search and the number is huge. Again this is a choice, but if you want to do an e-book you need to remember with the infinite number of books circulating, if you don't market your book it might never be found!

Marketing Books on the Internet

But even if you do market your book it may still never be found– so here are some suggestions. There are so many choices but we will just offer some to get you started
  Open a FaceBook page for you as the author and one for your book.
  Keep your followers updated often.
  Twitter is another place to get people to know about your book
  Are you good at making a video, try YouTube.
  How about Pinterest, Google+, Instagram, Reddit...
  Develop your own webpage, blog etc etc.etc. and so much more.....
There are so many possibilities, we have barely scratched the surface and that would probably take a whole book plus...!

Cooperative Publishing

   Another alternative to self-publishing is Cooperative Publishing. When you want to self-publish, but don't know how and need the expertise and services of a professional; Cooperative Publisher may be right for you. Cooperative Publishing uses the expertise of published authors, editors, marketers and a small press to assist the writer in each step of publishing, from an idea to YOUR PUBLISHED STORY, usually as much or as little as you need. Our authors have told us they liked Cooperative Publishing because they still had full control, but were being advised and guided by professionals. One of the features that our authors said helped them decide on Cooperative Publishing was that they could have their printed book within a short period of time, rather than waiting sometimes 18 months or more with a larger Publishing House. They were also happy to have someone sending out review copies, setting up book signings and web sites and doing other marketing, while they were choosing what they wanted to do. Most Cooperative Publishers will only take works they feel are marketable as their name will be listed as the publisher. This also makes your work more credible to the rest of the publishing world and if you wish, you can still continue to try to sell your book to another publisher. Remember: Even with Cooperative Publishing, you always own the copyright and the book is yours to do with as you choose.

So With so Many Choices-
We Suggest You Start Searching and See What Works Best For You!

But, Whatever You Decide,

it has been wonderful taking this Writing Journey with YOU and

REMEMBER: If you Have any Questions or Comments:

We Would Love to Hear From You!

email: info@goldenquillpress.com Subject line HTWYB–Questions/Comments

We Appreciate All Reviews and Referrals

From Your Three Wise Guides

WE WISH YOU GOOD WRITING AND MUCH SUCESS!

HOW TO WRITE YOUR BOOK From an Idea to YOUR PUBLISHED STORY   Take Your Story To Market

Writing Map 12

TRIP REVIEW

Map Directions

Learn All You Can About the Writing Industry & Your Genré
Submit A Properly Prepared Manuscript To The Right Editor
Use All the Resources Available — Libraries, Bookstores & The Internet
Treat Writing As A Business - Always Act As A Professional

Travel Instructions — Did You?

- ❑ Find your Genré

- ❑ Decide: Agent, Publisher, Self-Publishing, Cooperative Publishing

    Print on Demand, E-book, or just for Family and Friends

- ❑ Make Lists for marketing your work from Writer's Market, Literary

    Marketplace and Publisher's Weekly

- ❑ Use the Internet and Social Media

OUR WISE GUIDES
POINT YOU IN THE RIGHT DIRECTION

It's Wise to Know Who is publishing what and why

Editors Howl for a Growling Well done manuscript

Publishing is a Business - Helpful Authors can make their Book the leader of the pack!

◀ **NOTE** ▶
Walk past a Bookstore and Picture Your Book in the Window under the Title

BEST SELLER

HOW TO WRITE YOUR BOOK From an Idea to YOUR PUBLISHED STORY   Take Your Story To Market

Writing Map 12

TRACKING LOG

For _____
Book Name

Sent To:
_____   _____   _____
PUBLISHER   ADDRESS   ZIP CODE
_____   _____   _____   _____
EDITOR'S NAME   PASSED ON TO   TEL: #   FAX #
_____   _____   _____
EMAIL ADDRESS   DATE SENT   FOLLOW UP DATE
RESPONSE
ADDITIONAL INFORMATION

Sent To:
_____   _____   _____
PUBLISHER   ADDRESS   ZIP CODE
_____   _____   _____   _____
EDITOR'S NAME   PASSED ON TO   TEL: #   FAX #
_____   _____   _____
EMAIL ADDRESS   DATE SENT   FOLLOW UP DATE
RESPONSE
ADDITIONAL INFORMATION

Sent To:
_____   _____   _____
PUBLISHER   ADDRESS   ZIP CODE
_____   _____   _____   _____
EDITOR'S NAME   PASSED ON TO   TEL: #   FAX #
_____   _____   _____
EMAIL ADDRESS   DATE SENT   FOLLOW UP DATE
RESPONSE
ADDITIONAL INFORMATION

Sent To:
_____   _____   _____
PUBLISHER   ADDRESS   ZIP CODE
_____   _____   _____   _____
EDITOR'S NAME   PASSED ON TO   TEL: #   FAX #
_____   _____   _____
EMAIL ADDRESS   DATE SENT   FOLLOW UP DATE
RESPONSE
ADDITIONAL INFORMATION

GLOSSARY
Words Related to Writing

A

Advance – The amount paid to a writer by a publisher before a book is published. The advance is generally deducted from royalties earned from sales of the finished book.

Agent – A person who represents and acts on behalf of writers.

All rights – The rights contracted to a publisher (magazines, books) to permit the use of a writer's work any time, in any form without paying additional royalties.

Antagonists – A person (characters) who competes with or opposes another. An opponent or adversary.

Assignment – The contract between a writer and editor that confirms dates the writer will complete a project and fees to be paid the writer.

Autobiography – The story of one's own life written or dictated by oneself.

B

Book developer/packager – A business that plans and produces all elements of a book for publishers and producers.

Biography – An account of a person's life written by another.

By-line – The author's name on a published work.

C

Character – A person in a story or play.

Cliché – A trite expression or idea.

Climax – A decisive turning point or action.

Clips – Copies of a writer's work that has been published.

C

Confidant – The person to whom the main character would express undisclosed information the reader needs to know

Conflict – To clash or to be in opposition.

Contemporary – Relating to writing that reflects current trends, themes, and subjects.

Copy – Manuscript pages before being set in type.

Copy editing – The line by line editing of a manuscript.

Copyright – The lawful protection of a writer's work and considered to be in effect at the time of writing or by recording.

Cover letter – A one page, or brief letter to an editor sent with a manuscript.

D

Deadline – The date when a writer's work must be ready.

Denouement – The outcome, solution, or unraveling of a plot.

Description – Technique of describing or picturing by way of words.

Dialogue – The passages of talk or conversations in a play or story.

Disk copy – Circular plate on which data is stored; disk copy of a manuscript.

Draft – First or rough copies of a story, article, or other material.

E

Editing – To revise and make ready a manuscript

Editor – A person who's work is procuring and editing manuscripts

E-mail – Mail sent electronically by a computer.

Epiphany ending – The end of a story that gives the reader a sense of understanding and insight.

Exposition – The writing that explains facts, ideas, who characters are, the setting and

GLOSSARY

related information.

F

Fair use – A provision in copyright law that allows the use of short quotes or passages to be used from copyrighted work.

Fiction – A story or other work of the imagination and portraying imaginary characters and events.

First serial rights – The right to publish materials for the first time before it is in book form.

Flashback – Filling in details in a story to let the reader know something that happened in the past. Also called back story

Flash forward – A device in writing that prepares the reader for events to come without going into specific details. Also called foreshadowing.

Free writing – Unrestrained writing that allows ideas to flow. Also called clustering or brainstorming. Methods of generating fresh ideas.

G

Galleys – The first set of proofs of a manuscript before being prepared in page form.

Genré – A category or type of fiction: Horror, western, romance, science fiction, etc....

H

Hard copy – A copy of a manuscript printed from a computer.

H

Hook – The lead into a story that keeps the reader interested. To hook or grab interest.

I

Imprint – A publisher's line. Example: Jan, an imprint of Robin House Publishers.

J

Juvenile fiction – stories for children ages 2 to 12.

GLOSSARY

Justify – Printing in line or flush. As when typing a manuscript, you may not want to justify right margins.

L

Lead-in – The beginning of a new scene.

Lead time – The time between planning a book and the publication date.

Literary agent – The person who represents an author, finds a publisher and negotiates contracts.

M

Mainstream – Fiction that has a prevailing and strong trend.

Manuscript – An author's unpublished work in typewritten pages. Abbreviated ms or mss (plural).

Mass market – Books that appeal to a wide readership and are sold in various outlets such as grocery, stationary and drug stores.

Masthead – A list of a magazine's staff members, their titles and departments.

Metaphor – A figure of speech where a word or phrase used for one thing is applied to another as in imagery. Example: A snowfall of white beard covered the old man's face.

Multiple submissions – Submitting more than one story to the same editor at the same time.

N

Narration – The events in a story related by the person telling the story.

Narrator – The person who tells a story.

O

One-time rights – Permission to reprint an author's work one time only.

Opposition – A person who resists, has an opposite stance or contradicts another.

Outline – A summary of a story or book contents.

P

Pace – The slowing down or speeding up of a story by punctuation, dialogue, or the author's style and use of language.

Pen name – Pseudonym an author chooses to use to conceal his or her own name.

Plot – The events scheme or plan of a story through which characters progress.

Premise – A short explanation of what the story is about.

Proofreading – The careful reading and correcting of errors in a manuscript using proofreader's marks.

Proposal – An offer to write a specific work.

Protagonist – The lead character in a story; the hero.

Public domain – Written material that is no longer copyrighted or has never been copyrighted.

Q

Query letter (a letter of inquiry) – A type of cover letter, usually one page, written to an editor in which the writer proposes a story, book, article, or an idea to the editor.

R

Rejection slip – A note from a publishing house that accompanies the return or refusal of an author's work.

Reprint rights – The right of a publisher to print an article or other work after it has been printed by another publication.

Resolution – The solution to a problem. A decision for future action. The end of a story made clear by an explanation.

Revision – To read carefully and correct, improve, update, or change a manuscript or other writing.

Royalties – A specified percentage paid for the work of an author.

S

SASE – Self addressed stamped envelope sent by an author for the return of work not accepted for publication.

Setting – The time period and location in which a story takes place.

Simultaneous submissions – Sending copies of a manuscript to more than one publisher at the time.

Simile – A figure of speech in which one thing is likened to another. Example: "A river of tears" or "Tears flowed like a river."

Slant – Writing a topic with a different approach.

Slush-pile – The stack of unsolicited manuscripts not likely to be accepted by a publisher.

Subplot – The secondary story running thread-like through the main plot.

Subsidiary rights – All the rights in addition to or other than book rights a published author may agree upon.

Synopsis – A brief summary of a story, usually a page or two, written to interest the editor in the complete work.

T

Tag – The words following the quoted dialogue of a character. Example: "Where are you?" he asked. "I am at the store," she said.

Theme – The central and dominant idea of a story or other work, also called the back-bone, the message, or main thread.

Tone – The manner of writing that shows the attitude of the narrator.

Transition – A word, phrase, sentence, or paragraph that relates a preceding topic to a succeeding one. The connecting of one idea to the next.

U

Unsolicited submissions – Manuscripts sent to a publisher without an agency representation or that an editor did not ask to see.

V

Viewpoint – The position from which the narrator tells the story and how the story's action is meant to be seen by the reader.

FINAL WORD FROM OUR AUTHORS

We traveled this long road together and now that we have completed our journey

We APPLAUD YOU!

You made a commitment and followed through; in spite of the bumpy roads,

difficult and unfamiliar terrain, detours and seemingly never ending miles.

Your finished story can now be the beginning of a new journey –

one that leads to new heights of accomplishment—

maybe even the best seller list.

As we leave you at your final destination we remind you that

Many such successful journeys are possible

The techniques you've learned in this book will hopefully provide the tools

for many successful adventures

You are only limited by your own imagination

We look forward to traveling with you again!

If this book was helpful, Please Tell Others & Post Reviews On-line

And now a word from Our Three Wise Guides:

ALERT— ALERT!

**Our Wise Writing Guides AGREE
You are a BEST SELLER in OUR BOOK!**

Thank you for traveling with us ..."From an Idea to YOUR PUBLISHED STORY."

AUTHORS BIOGRAPHIES

**Francine Barish-Stern** has been an author for over 40 years, and has received numerous awards for poetry and short stories. Her "Rainbow City" won first place and was published in "The Arts Newspaper." She has been a writer for newspapers and magazines and authored numerous books including, "TELL IT TO THE FUTURE" and "NEW HORIZONS." She has recently created her first full length novel as a trilogy, "Code 47 to B R EV Force." Francine has developed writing programs for all ages and has edited books for authors of all ages. She tutors writers and teaches writing classes, acting and co-wrote and produced, the play, "The WE Nobody Knows" for Crown Players. Also an accomplished business writer, she has specialized in seminars on telemarketing. Francine has recently added photography to her creative interests and has won major awards for her exhibits. Her photograph, "Falls at the Bridge" created as Art on Gold, was exhibited at the Art Museum of Western Virginia, and her "Southern Calm took first place in an art festival for mixed media. All her art work are produced exclusively as Art on Gold, and she has written a full line of greeting cards, called Greetings on Gold.

**Bobbi R. Madry**, Educational Director for The Write Source and Golden Quill Press also serves as consultant, author and editor. During her career which has spanned more than 30 years, she has also served as senior editor of numerous books and educational publications for major New York City publishers. She has also written book reviews for national magazines. Bobbi served as Associate Publisher for a New York newspaper where she also mentored aspiring writers. She has received numerous awards for writing and community service. Bobbi teaches writing and poetry and holds degrees in the Arts and Behavioral Sciences. Her published works: Human Relations For Business - A Vocational Dictionary - The Job Seeker's Guide - Love Makes The Difference - Work Force 2000 (co-author) - The Professional Models Handbook (co-author). She has been the co-author and editor for "Tell it to the Future" and "New Horizons" as well as the editor of hundreds of works. She is presently authoring several new books.

Books By Golden Quill Press

BUY AT www.goldenquillpress.com

CODE 47 to BREV Force
By: F. Barish-Stern

Book 1

Cracko

Book 2

QuizMaster & MixMatcher

Book 3

Controller

The adventures of The BREV Force: A computer virus has invaded the world and set its "sites" on an army of mindless students to do its bidding. Fighting this force and its holograms is the task taken on by the Kane Family. Evie and Brad Kane, college students watching their friends becoming obedient foot soldiers, decide to do something about it, but it backfires and the BREV Force is born. But more than that is born and now it is up to them to find a way to defeat CONTROLLER and keep the world safe.

TELL IT TO THE FUTURE
BY: Francine R. Cefola (F.Barish-Stern) & Bobbi R. Madry

TELL IT TO THE FUTURE—Have I Got A Story For You ... about the Century leaves personal messages with timelines and stories about our hopes, dreams, or events that impacted on, or changed our lives. Each story focuses on events from a specific decade of the twentieth century with descriptions that reflect the color of the times. Some are witty, some filled with wisdom, while others pull at your heart strings.

HOW TO WRITE YOUR BOOK…
From an Idea to YOUR PUBLISHED STORY
BY: Bobbi Madry & Francine Barish-Stern

An Interactive Journey to writing your finished and published story. For anyone who writes or wants to write. This workbook will walk you through all the stages of writing and will support you with tips, forms, and guidelines, Our Three Writing Guides will give you their expertise, as they take this fun and exciting journey with you. Personal assistance is also available from writing and publishing professionals.

COMPASSION'S LURE
BY: Kathleen Lukens

This is the story of a visionary. Kathy Lukens founder of Camp Venture - advocate for all people with special needs stood up for the rights and deeds of those who could not fight for themselves. With words backed by tireless efforts, Kathy made the impossible happen for the developmentally disabled- a home and the proper attention to their needs. She was truly one of the Great Women of our times.

NEW HORIZONS -
Life's Poetic Connections
BY: Francine R. Cefola (F. Barish-Stern) & Bobbi R. Madry

Poetry is the art that speaks to our hearts and minds. Like a beautiful painting or a musical composition, this collection of poetry will take you into worlds limited only by your imagination... from the splendor of a sunset to tasting candy, to memories from a rocking chair ... **Let These Poems Take You To Your Own New Horizons!!**

the GRANPA SPIDER stories
BY: Granpa Spider

A delightful story for children of all ages. Granpa Spider weaves a web of adventure and intrigue, mystery and fun! Along with his Arachnid friends, Penelope, The Colonel, and others we journey into the exciting world of the web. As Shamrock McGee says, "May wind be at your web. May your web be in the trees. May cicada be chattering. May there be a host of bees, And, may the web that you spin be serving all your needs... "

LOVE MAKES A DIFFERENCE -
BY: Mary Bianchini and Bobbi Madry

Arriving as an immigrant with her mother in the early 1900's, Mary grew up to become one of the most influential figures in Rockland County, N.Y. Honored by four Presidents and in the Congressional Record, Mary shares her advice about family, community service and reaching her dreams.

THE POEM BOOK

BY: Daniel Windheim

A brain injury victim of a car accident young Daniel Windheim's life is turned upside down. He turns to poetry to express his frustration, anger and and to take the reader on a beautiful journey through recuperation and new life challenges. Daniel Windheim is truly a shining hero, overcoming life's worst experience. "I remain practical; but a realist, and accept what I am.
Life is good, and there is goodness in life."

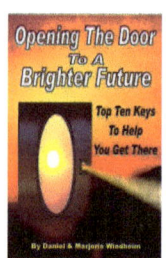
OPENING THE DOOR TO A BRIGHTER FUTURE
BY: Daniel Windheim

This book grew out of the experiences of my son, Dan, sustaining a traumatic brain injury and the efforts he made to recover and build a productive life, we decided that many of the lessons both Dan and I learned from that experience might have relevance to others recovering from injuries or illnesses. We therefore set out to write a book detailing ten key strategies that could help individuals in their recovery efforts and to share the experiences of some survivors as they struggle to return to a healthy life.

MAE SINGS ABOUT SHORT VOWELS

BY: Karen A. Coleman

"Mae Sings About Short Vowels," was developed by Karen Coleman, as a method for teaching music, while learning vowel sounds. The book uses songs and a vowel recognition technique in an interactive way to help students improve reading skills while learning musical notes

CHALLENGING MESSAGES FROM BEYOND

BY: Marjorie Struck

Does the Spiritual World have a message for us? Can we learn to understand that communication? Marjorie Struck certainly believes. This is her personal story of how a message form Beyond changed her life. Informative, at times shocking, but ultimately a journey that reveals a side of the spiritual world that can transform you-forever. Marjorie invites you along to witness how this revelation helped her understand the connection between life and beyond- and how souls in the after life help us to find the Light!

THERE IS HOPE

BY: Debby Paine

There Is Hope is a collection of religious poetry about the struggles, pains questions and fears we all face. Debby's love of family, church and community is portrayed as she searches for and reaches toward God to find hope. These poems from the heart-for the heart, will reach out to everyone searching for hope. " Reach for it. Hold on to it.
'Hope is There.' "

SWEET MERCY

BY: Rebecca H. Cofer

Katherine Ryder peels away the decades of family secrets to tell her story of growing up in Fairburn, Georgia at the turn of the century - 1900. She battles many obstacles to free herself from small town life and her autocratic mother and moves to Atlanta. In the big city she is betrayed by the man she loves. But her generous heart and hard work pay off, bringing her joy and fulfillment in the end.

Other books marketed by Golden Quill Press:

YOU ARE WHAT YOU WEAR
BY:William Thourlby

"First impressions" are lasting. YOU ARE WHAT YOU WEAR will help you make the right "first impression." Develop skills that are cost effective because they not only increase the quality of life in the workplace, contribute to employee morale and embellish the company image, they play a major role in developing a person's self image and generating profits. The lack of these skills can be highly visible and costly for any person or company in every day and age.

PASSPORT TO POWER

BY: William Thourlby

Part practical, part primer, part visionary, Passport to Power, gives the reader background and formulas to follow to acquire and master international communication skills and provide the keys to unlocking human potential for success as a leader in the new global village of today.

TELL IT TO THE FUTURE

Have I got A Story For You…
About the Twentieth Century

Stories to make

You laugh, Stories to make

You cry

Stories to bring

Back memories of a Time Gone By

Stories of a time that

Most of us never knew

Coming to America…

Going off to war

Just to name a few

These stories vividly paint a portrait of America during the decades

Of the 20th Century…

Am America you'll never forget

GREAT REFERENCE and RESOURCE Book
For the Twentieth Century

BE SURE YOU
TELL IT TO THE FUTURE

Order at www.goldenquillpress.com
Or inquire at info@goldenquillpress.com

www.ingramcontent.com/pod-product-compliance
Lightning Source LLC
Chambersburg PA
CBHW061119010526
44112CB00024B/2912